Free *video* Class

Break Patterns. Start Connecting.

Get Instant Access At

www.KamalaChambers.com

ROAD to LOVE

Lessons and Love Letters
from a Journey to Intimacy

Road to Love

Lessons and Love Letters from a Journey to Intimacy

By: Kamala Chambers

Published By:

www.PromotingNaturalHealth.com

Printed in the United States of America

ISBN-10: 0-9906462-3-8

ISBN-13: 978-0-9906462-3-5

Table of Contents

INTRODUCTION

The subsequent letters follow my love affairs and travels, which have led me to discover the essence of intimacy. Along the way, I offer roadmaps to uncover how to apply intimacy to your relationships and be turned on by life. The letters are about true events and people—only the names have been changed. You can choose to read just the letters, just the lessons, or both, as you work your way through this journey.

The most fundamental key to intimacy is simple presence, without stories of who you are or who someone else is. When people are given permission to be radically honest, express desires, touch and be touched, say "yes" and "no" without justification, and love their own "ugliness"—intimacy is easy and love happens.

Throughout this entire book, the practice of taking deep breaths could very well be the most valuable lesson. Being aware of your breath and body will keep calling you home to the moment. If you're unwilling to breathe deeply, you might as well put this book down right now. Your breath is key to intimacy. You might say, "I already know I need to take deep breaths!" Of course you do. And it is something that requires continual practice.

I invite you to be aware of your body as much as

possible while reading these pages. Keep asking yourself, "How can I relax more deeply right now?" When you're relaxed and breathing deeply, there are many magical and physiological phenomena that occur. We'll get into those later in the book. As you breathe and relax your body while reading this book, let the information sink in. Now, take a deep breath.

ONE

EASTON
Fully Trusting Yourself
and Your Partner

At the age of 15, I met my first love. Our connection was instant and powerful, and changed the way I saw the world. With him, my body was able to access profound levels of pleasure and tap into a sense of unity.

We decided to spend a summer hitch-hiking around the United States. In three months, we traveled through 20 states and had to rely solely on each other, our intuition, the kindness of others and trust in the universe to make our way. Together we learned a lifetime of how to experience each moment to the fullest. In the end, we were ripped from one another and I was left struggling to cope with the pain of loss.

Through these letters, and the lessons that I learned from my experiences, I aim to offer you a guide that shows how to fully trust yourself and those you love.

Opening to Pleasure

Dear Easton,

We're in the quiet of your studio. The windows are open, and the warm January night air carries in the sound of rain falling in the alleyway. The night spilling in feels warm like some blue green heat wave in the middle of winter.

You have no furniture, except one tiny ragged couch. Next to me, you strum and sing a song about a gypsy thief. I had no idea nylon, wood, and voice could penetrate me so deeply.

Without looking at me, you set down your guitar and lay your head against my breasts. With the soft of my finger, I trace your mango lips. I yearn to taste your salty sweetness.

The night finally takes over and we crawl into the darkness of the closet, where you keep your bed. There is no light in here, not even the dimmest glow. It's darker than the faces that linger in the alleyway below.

In your arms, I become a writer. My body blank pages. Your body, the pen, writing a story of love into me. My pages quickly fill with the black ink of this night. In the defining darkness, I feel like I belong. My virgin body effortlessly takes you in. I cradle you inside me. The emptiness floods with color. My heart spills its truth in slight whimpers. We say nothing. We see nothing. We feel everything in this pitch black cavern.

Our story is written in my cells now,

Kamala

Intimacy calls us not only into deep connection with another, but also with ourselves. Intimacy is about engaging with the pleasurable pulse of life. It's about feeling the pleasurable flow of energy that pulses through all things. When you are intimately engaged with life, everything you experience is enjoyable—the wind brushing your skin, the prolonged eye contact with the cashier, even the sting of heartbreak. It is all magnificent.

When everything is pleasurable, we don't experience the pain of losing pleasure. It is said that all suffering comes from attachment or aversion. If you are always experiencing the pleasure of each sensation, you don't become attached or have aversion to "good" or "bad" feelings.

Explore how deeply you can open to pleasure. Let the mundane become sensual and allow your entire body to penetrate and be penetrated by the universe.

Roadmap to Intimacy—Opening to Pleasure

1. Allow yourself to rest alone in a comfortable position.

2. Take slow deep breaths. As you exhale, breathe all the way down your body and into your feet. As you inhale, breathe all the way from your feet up to the top of your head.

3. Consider that there is a wave of energy that comes up from the earth and pulses all the way up your legs, up your torso, and out the top of your head.

   Now feel that wave moving from your head, down your torso and legs and out the bottom of your feet. This wave ideally would be a slow steady pulse like a gentle ocean tide or move like a long steady breath. If your body is constricted or you shut off parts of you, like your pelvis or your heart, then the wave can't pulse all the way through you.

4. Notice how your body feels. Notice where your body or your breath might feel constricted. What is enjoyable about this experience?

5. Notice what parts of your body have pleasurable sensations. Allow your breath to move into the areas of your body that feel pleasure. Allow your breath to heighten whatever pleasure you're experiencing.

6. Either journal about what you discovered or share with a partner.

Being Present to Who Someone Is

Dear Easton,

We buy two one-way tickets from Washington State to Pennsylvania. The Greyhound is overcrowded as we board in downtown Tacoma. There are only two seats left. One seat at the front and one seat at the back. As I sit down next to a stranger, I wonder if this is a metaphor for how our trip will go...separated as we journey in the same direction.

We watch the familiar landscape of the city slip by outside the window until the starkly familiar buildings become a whirl of all new passing excitement. We'll spend three days and four nights on the Greyhound, attentively peering out windows, hurrying through fifteen minute breaks at fast food restaurants, bus shuffling, and napping.

I dream about the people we've left behind and the new places we'll find. We reach Idaho in a great stretch across seemingly endless flatness. Rolling hills gracefully stand on the horizon. The clouds shift to create colorful dreams. As I watch them churn, I know this is what I've longed for.

Our time out here, out in the open, is short compared to the time spent in confinement. The majestic simplicity of heavenly rays as the sun bursts through clouds now carries insight. Already I am gaining perspective on my life.

You've been carrying around Tacoma like a noose. It's been weighing heavily on both of us. It's hard to learn anything new when there is nothing new around us to learn from. We've been so uninspired seeing the same thing every day. For weeks, I've been watching your tall slender body bent over canvases, trying to paint your pain away. And I've been scouring those images hoping to understand who you are.

The very first moment I saw you, I knew I loved you. I knew nothing would ever be the same, and yet I feel I am only now getting to know you.

The farther we get from the life we left behind, the more perspective I gain. The clouds part in my mind and the sun of insight spills through. I am able to create more when I see more, and when I see more, I learn more.

This is why we must hit the road,

Kamala

When we first get to know someone, there is often a testing process we go through to decide how much we can open up to the other person. If people pass our tests, then the aperture of how much we open widens. This process makes sense. We've all been hurt, and we don't want to be hurt again.

Logically it makes sense to keep our walls up until we feel it is safe and the other won't hurt us. But there are consequences to building walls. Walls can keep us from feeling pain, but they can also keep us from feeling love.

Our walls are erected from our past pains and hurts. When we interact with people from a closed off space, as the same person we've always been, we continue attracting the same old pain. Our whole lives are a process of patterns repeating. If we consider it normal for people to put us down all the time, we'll probably continue to attract people who put us down.

In the moments we are present, we have the joy of being surprised by others. I'm sure you've met someone before and felt an instant connection. It is in that instant when our views of the world expand and our ideas about who and what we are begin to stretch like taffy. It is magic. In those moments we step out of our ideas about how the world is and into the truth of what the present is offering. We see the world through the clear lens that only being in the moment can bring.

These kismet moments evoke us to tear down who we

think we are and step into who we are becoming. These moments invite us to see a person for who they are, and not who we want them to be.

There is something profoundly powerful when we meet someone with willingness to fall completely in love with them exactly as they are. We can walk through our lives having these kismet meetings every day. We can be aligned with whatever gifts each person is shining without the fear and questions of who this person is or is going to become to us.

When you're relaxed in your body, you become present and know that each moment holds a world of opportunities. You don't miss those truly magical moments of kismet meetings. The people you love in the first moments of meeting can be some of the most significant people in your life. It will feel like you already know these people in the first seconds of meeting them.

Having the sense you know someone upon meeting them can feel like love at first sight. When you allow yourself to be immersed in the moment, this experience can take a hold of you. It can make you feel like you've been scooped up and spun in a silken cocoon. It can make life as you've known it come screeching to a halt. It can send pulsing waves deeply through your body and rearranges your cells. It shakes you until you know nothing will ever be the same again.

We'll know we're experiencing lust at first sight, instead

of love, when we crave the other like a drug. When we are overrun by lust, we can lose our sense of what is real, which causes us to become sloppy with our boundaries. We move from being present and seeing who someone is to seeing them for who we want them to be.

You'll know you are being present to others and yourself when:

→ your thoughts are focused on the moment
→ you are aware of your body
→ you clearly see and take in your surroundings
→ you are centered and grounded
→ your feelings are about what is in front of you

To be present to a person or situation, sometimes we need to make some space. By finding ways to fulfill what the other person provides us, we become less reliant on needing that person to meet our needs. Stepping back and giving to ourselves can give us a chance to see them with fresh eyes.

Sometimes it is difficult to see the truth of a person or situation when we're fully immersed. How can we step back and see the whole forest when we're lost in the trees? It is often easy to fall in love with someone before we really know them because we can see them from a vantage perspective. As we get closer to others, it can be challenging to see the whole array of who they are. As we get closer, we see them for who they've been. Not who they are showing up as in this moment. When we take a step back from a situation or person, it allows us the opportunity to see the situation as a whole.

Roadmap to Intimacy—Being Present To What Is

1. Think of a situation or person you're struggling with.

2. Journal or share with a partner three things that this person or situation is providing you.

3. Journal or share with a partner three ways you can take space from this person or situation for an entire day. (Give yourself more time if you need it.)

4. Throughout the day, think about ways you can give yourself what the person or situation gives you.

5. At the end of the day, take five minutes to quietly reflect on the situation or person. Ask yourself what this situation is calling you to see.

Fully Trusting Yourself—Breathe

Dear Easton,

You and I spend a week at the National Rainbow Peace Gathering, muddy and crazed in the woods with thousands of dazed seekers. We have no idea what we're doing now, but we know it's time to crawl out of the forest and leave the drum circles and pot clouds behind.

It's a long slippery path back to the road. The mud cakes to our bare feet forming heavy dirt moccasins that buffer our soles from the jagged ground. Once we get to the gravel road, we scribble in blue ink on torn cardboard, "We need a ride to a faraway place." Dirt stained hitchhikers line the road, all with signs to specific cities. We have no idea where we're going. I feel the buoyancy of not having a destination. We sit for about an hour until a pickup stops.

A bearded man in his fifties leans out of his duct tape window. "Is Missouri far enough away for you?"

I pull out the already crinkled U.S. map that I tore from one of my dad's books. Where the hell is Missouri?

Looks good to me, I grin once I locate it.

No other words are exchanged. We haul our bags into the

back of the covered truck and climb in. We pile on top of a mountain of his gear. As he slams the tailgate behind us, the elation of being out of the sun is quickly overshadowed by the backflips of the unknown stirring in my belly. My grin towards you is my attempt to hide the fear.

As the truck jostles along, the breeze creeping from the broken window puts me at ease. I feel good being on the road again. I trace the memories of the gathering and can't seem to shake the sounds of the perpetual drumming from my mind.

Through the dusty windows, green trees speed by in a blur. We drive all day and into the night, and drift off to the quiet hum of the road. We drive for an infinite amount of time without stopping and attempt to sleep off the drugs on the lumpy bed of gear.

Advertisements in neon splashes smear against the dark sky. We follow yellow dotted lines and headlight lit signs. We leave blackness behind us and speed toward unknown destinations. Car wheels on smooth pavement become a freedom lullaby, singing us to sleep.

We wake to the back of the truck banging open with no idea how many days or lifetimes we've been driving for. As we uncurl our bodies from the truck, a desolate campsite comes into focus.

Everyone stretches out of the truck silently. The driver builds a small fire. Wordlessly we lay our sleeping bags down. You and I snuggle next to each other. A crescent moon looms on the horizon. Everyone easily drifts off. You're breathing softly with the rhythm of sleep. I lay awake wondering what adventures lay ahead, thousands of miles from what I've known. The blinding sky is crowded with so many stars; it's too much to take in. The vastness and brilliance so overwhelming, I choke on my own breath. Afraid I might fall into the stars, I wrap my arms around you as if you'll keep me from being sucked in.

Where are we?

A phosphorescent shooting star answers in a language I somehow understand. Gulping in another breath, my body starts to settle into the unpadded ground.

We're going to be okay,

Kamala

When we are breathing, we're not creating stories. Our breath is one of our most simple and effective tools to calm down the nervous system and open us more fully. If we are breathing deeply, we can't be lost in stories. Our breath will keep inviting us back to the moment.

When we are in a state of fear or isolation or anger or anticipation, the first thing we do is hold our breath. When we breathe deeply, we trick our bodies into thinking there is no danger. It is not about calming our nervous systems down at every moment, but it is about creating an appropriate response to whatever is approaching. The best way to invite ourselves back into the moment and lull ourselves into a state of calm is with the breath. When our nervous system is hijacked by fear, anxiety, anger or distrust, we don't have room to open and experience intimacy.

Breath is the gateway to love and the dial for our nervous systems. If we want our nervous system to calm into a state of openness and connection, we deepen our breath. If we breathe fast and shallow, our nervous systems will respond as though we are in danger. In order to truly connect with another, we have to open by breathing. When we breathe deeply and share non-agenda touch with another, the brain releases oxytocin, the chemical that creates a sense of bonding. When the calming connected feeling of oxytocin moves down into our genitals, that sense of bonding connects us to the core of who we are.

Breathing is a necessary way of flowing energy through

your body. Breath can awaken you to the present moment and clear the mind. Breathing deeply might be difficult for you if you're not used to it. The more you practice, the easier it will become. The muscles needed to help you breathe more deeply will develop as you practice.

When exploring the breath, think about the edges of yourself. Think about softening your arms and legs. Consider how effortless you can make the breath. When your belly and chest are like a balloon, there is a certain amount of force necessary to expand and contract. There is a deeper practice of expanding your breath to every part of your body. When you let your breath softly flow to every cell in your body, there is an organic and deeply intimate experience with yourself that can come alive. Letting your breath curl its way to your limbs, you move out of the struggle to deepen your breath, and into the feeling that your body is being breathed.

Roadmap to Intimacy—Breath

♥ Try playing with the dial of your breath.

♥ Notice how you're breathing right now without trying to change it. Pay attention to how relaxed or
contracted your body feels. How much of your body
are you aware of right now?

♥ Now what happens when you deepen your breath?
What happens when you breathe all the way into
your belly? Allow your limbs to soften and notice
what happens when you breathe into your arms and
legs. Do you notice the constriction in your body
shifting? Do you notice your own awareness or alert-
ness shifting? Notice how you open as you breathe.

♥ If you are connecting to a partner, synchronize your
breath with your partner's breath. If they are breathing shallowly, mock their breath and slowly start
breathing deeper. They will naturally fall into har-
mony with your breath.

We Need Each Other

Dear Easton,

You and I wander through a desolate train yard. You tell me the first train we see, we'll just jump on. I'm kicking along with a heavy feeling weighing me down, a strange blend of hopelessness and excitement.

And then we hear it. The familiar screech of an approaching train.

Is this train stopping? How do we know where it's going?

I might as well have said nothing. You ignore my questions and dash toward the train. I follow you the way I followed my older brothers when they were about to do something stupid.

The noisy steel beast wails in at a swift crawl. Its rumble rattles inside me as we sprint alongside it. Closed boxcar after closed boxcar passes. You're scanning for an opening. You holler towards me. The last car is empty.

Even at full sprint we can just barely keep up with the train. You sling off your small pack, toss it into the boxcar, and struggle to pull yourself up into the speeding train. You're a foot taller than me. I try to comprehend how I'm going to make it.

I am running as fast as I can, my oversized backpack

weighing me down. I trip over the rails. At last, one hand catches up and grabs onto the edge of the vibrating boxcar. It's the height of my shoulder. I don't see any footholds, just this tall speeding platform atop bone-splintering wheels. I struggle and try to lift myself awkwardly. I couldn't have lifted myself onto a platform this high if it was stationary and I wasn't carrying a pack.

I look up at you in that boxcar. You're fulfilling a dream. You're finally hopping trains. You're perched up there like it's your purpose. In the midst of my panic, I feel a pulse of happiness for you. I know this is what you've been waiting for.

I huff and cling to the side of the train. You grab my hand and desperately try to pull me up. With this heavy pack and the speed of the train, like a punch in the gut, I realize there is no way I'm going to make it. I stumble. The train starts to get away from me.

Our eyes meet. We both know I'm not going to make it. This will be the last time I ever see you, riding away to some better place. The moment lasts an eternity. There are these key moments in life where everything stands still and there is a critical crossroad—when the next choice will shift fate forever. This is one of those moments. Our entire love affair flashes before me. It's all been leading to this point, this inevitable goodbye.

I watch you as you speed away from me. We silently gaze into *one another. This is the last time we'll ever see each other. You're fulfilling your dream, and I can't keep up. The train flattens my heart like a penny as I watch you roll away. It grinds in the wheels of that unforgiving beast. Still running, still staring into one another, the caboose passes me by. In that infinite moment, I say goodbye.*

And then, you just jump off. We say nothing. We walk away from the train tracks in silence. My head is down in shame. I'm holding you back. Why did you jump off? Why didn't you keep going? You've been wanting this for so long and now you're just walking away. For what? I am overwhelmed with the sting of failure taunting me.

It hits me. You chose me over that dream. In that moment, even through the pain of letting you down, I realize that we're in this together. You love me in a way that I couldn't see before.

With the potential of you leaving, I see how vulnerable I am now. Fifteen years old, over two thousand miles from home, with empty pockets and a backpack full of tie-dye. I need you way more than I will ever admit. And I think you need me too.

We never go back to the train tracks. We never even talk about it. From then on, every time we hear a train though, we both wonder what it would be like to be on it.

We're in this together now,

Kamala

We need others no matter how self-sufficient we want to be. The people we love hold the keys to the deepest parts of us. We need others to access more of who we are. If we isolate ourselves and try to work things out alone, we don't have the gift of another showing us our blind spots.

With others, we practice how to trust. We can practice sharing ourselves, and loving ourselves, no matter how people are responding. When you are intimate with others, everything that is in the way of love will come up to be released. It's so incredibly beautiful and vulnerable to be fully intimate with another human being.

The deeper we move into intimacy, the more our inner obstacles arise. Intimacy invites us to burn through the obstacles that hold us back from expressing trust and heart and feelings. We're invited again and again to open, relax and be received by ourselves…and possibly even the person in front of us.

Each person we open ourselves to hands us a key to unlock otherwise hidden parts of ourselves. Being intimate with another gives us new opportunities to love ourselves. When we become more intimate with another, the emotional obstacles stored in our own bodies might start to surface. All the history, fears, stories, and beliefs will float up because we finally give them space it come to the surface.

When things are floating up, the most important lesson to remember is breathing deeply. Simply notice what is happening within our own bodies. As long as we keep breathing, there is space for our own distorted stories and beliefs to burn away. If we stop breathing and clamp down on a story, it gets projected onto others. The degree to which we're resisting relaxation and openness is the degree to which we are still holding onto our belief systems, stories, and past hurts.

Whatever we constrict around will get projected onto others. If we're not making space inside of ourselves for who we are moment by moment, we'll try to find someone outside of ourselves who can hold that aspect of who we are. As soon as we start projecting onto someone else rather than fully owning our feelings, we lose the power to change the issue. The behavior and actions of others can then dictate our own beliefs, feelings, and reactions. Often we give the power of our own thoughts and feelings away.

Each person offers a reflection of what is alive and waiting to be awakened within ourselves. But sometimes we give our power away to strangers. We see someone who turns us on, and rather than feeling that attraction within ourselves, we make the attraction solely about the other person. Maybe that person smiles at us and we create a story that we are wanted by that person. Maybe we get together with them and that person cheats, leaving us devastated. We thought we loved this person, but there was no room for actual love because the space was occupied by projections. We gave them power to hurt us by not owning within ourselves the beliefs, love and fears we were projecting onto them.

When we tap into intimacy, we move out of our projections, calm our nervous systems and deeply connect with what we are experiencing in this moment. The deeper we breathe, the more space we create in our own bodies for what is true moment by moment.

Roadmap to Intimacy—Deepening Trust

The next time you notice yourself feeling strong emotions like fear, anger, or hurt, slow everything down. Take a moment to notice what you're feeling in your body. Take a pause with yourself and notice whatever you might be needing right now. Let yourself know that whatever it is that you need in this moment is welcome. The more you take space and time to be with your feelings, the easier it will be to trust yourself. You'll build self-trust in knowing that you're going to be there for you, no matter what.

Spending time looking into your partner's eyes is a great way to build trust in a relationship. It's a way to let your partner know that you need each other without being needy. Eye gazing before, during, and after sex is a way to recognize the beauty and divinity within you as it is reflected back to you by your lover. Making eye contact may seem like the simplest act, but it can open you to some of the most profound experiences, transporting you into a feeling of deep trust and unity.

Drinking in What Each Moment Offers

Dear Easton,

You and I fall in love with Zion right away. Our love for the place amplifies our already overwhelming love for each other. We wake to huge towering rock formations telling us stories of the past, and we make our way toward Angels Landing, a long hike up a seemingly endless ascension of switchbacks. By the time we're at the top, I can't tell if my breath is gone from the hefty climb, from the views, or from the sudden-death drop offs on both sides of the narrow trail. Standing on top of this peak that was just towering over us, peering deeply into valleys, I feel truly free.

For years I will be haunted by this place. Each recollection will stir up these piercing views as lucid as today. And with the memory, a feeling will flood me that I can only sum up as magic. The kind of magic that spills in when you've hiked hard and long and your body is high with breath. The kind that happens when you've finally gone as far as you can go, you step to the edge, and the whole world unfolds in the view.

It's nothing like a scenic outlook where you pull your car over and take a picture out the half cracked window. This is the kind of view you have to win. You have to battle an impossibly steep incline and feel the weight of the pack and the pain of every step. You battle the churning thoughts that have been waiting for such an occasion to well up. It's the kind of victory you don't know you're celebrating until you're pushed right up to the edge. In the post war of the climb, all that's left is shaking muscles and adrenaline holding you from falling off the ledge. One more step and you'll be back to where you started in an instant.

It's as if I've never looked before, never really seen anything until this moment. The world has opened up and we drink in the colors of the valley below, of the mountains at eye level, of the clouds we can stretch a hand to touch.

This is the kind of magic that will reach through time and grab ahold of me at any age. This moment will forever be tangible—immortalized by memory and imprinted like a passport stamp with your name on it. This moment holds so much more than a pretty view.

We are opened into some great mystery, and we don't shrink back. We free dive this one together. The crimson rock, the impossibly blue sky, the expanse in every direction, the touch of your hand against my lower back, the taste of sweat on my upper lip. These will hang on me always. Our love moves through time *and creates the Virgin River that carved out these canyons. Our love tints the sky and stains these rocks red with our hearts.*

Our love will reverberate through this valley like an echo that never ends,

Kamala

Take a deep breath.

Now feel the air touching your skin, hear the buzz of your environment, notice the sensations in your belly, taste your own lips. Just like your breath, sensations can keep drawing you back to the present. Your sensations will continuously beckon you home, back to the moment.

We live in a culture of sensory assault. The price checkers screaming over the intercom, under fluorescent lights, in Walmart. Processed foods loaded with MSG that makes it impossible to taste more subtle flavors. The flashing images of commercials. The reek of chemical perfumes. The screech of traffic. The bombardments of perpetual sounds and sights are simply too much for the mind to process.

When our senses are overwhelmed, it is incredibly challenging to stay in our bodies and in the moment. Our senses process more information than our conscious minds can take in. Therefore, the body holds a wisdom that the mind doesn't have.

Our senses connect us with our bodies. They are messengers. Have body pain? Listen to it. It has insight into the subconscious aspects of you. It is through our senses that we become aware of simple things and engage more in the moment. When you feel the wind against your skin, let bird songs fill your ears, smell the crispness of the air, you are in the moment. Only here and now can we engage in the richness of what life is offering.

There really is no right or wrong, there is simply what is going on in your own body moment by moment. There is no bad or good way to feel—there are simply sensations. It's when we are attached to the sensations or try to push them away that we create pain for ourselves.

When we stay curious about what is coming up, we can actually get the messages that our bodies are trying to tell us. When a contraction comes up, approach it with an inquiry. "Oh that's interesting. What does this want to tell me?" And just notice your thoughts, feelings, breath, and sensations.

You don't need to figure out why you are feeling what you're feeling. You don't need to shut it off. Your only job is to notice it and discover what is actually true about the experience.

Roadmap to Intimacy—Waking Up Senses

Approach everything with childlike amazement. Pretend you are a child trying everything for the first time. When you go to bite into an apple, do it as though you've never tasted an apple before. Not only that, look at that apple as though it is the greatest gift you've ever been given. You'll be amazed at what you can taste and feel when you are fully engaging with what's in front of you.

Practice waking up your senses with a partner. Pay attention to the subtleties of how your partner smells, tastes, and feels. How does the skin of their inner arm feel on the back of your fingers? All those tiny sensations invite you into a most delicious now. Practice tuning into the minute details of your beloved.

Intuitive Living

Dear Easton,

The mouth of Bourbon Street opens and grins its cobblestone smile at us. It's narrow and perfect, like a cultured dream. At the entrance sits a lone black man singing his own wake song into the saxophone. I squeal. I had no idea what to expect out of this city of blues, but it's just like I imagined it to be. Serendipitously, on the other upturned corner of Bourbon Street's smile is a lone pay-phone. The scene is too perfect to go unshared.

As if the boiling over tomato soup of my enthusiasm will somehow bleed through the phone lines and spoon feed my father reassurance, I pick up the receiver and place the call. Collect. I can hardly hear the faint answer at the other end over the blaring of sax, but I know it's my dad who answers.

I don't hesitate, "Hear that?"

I hold the sticky receiver into the humid southern air, and let my dad sop up the sounds of bluesy delight.

"Guess where I am!" Trying to make my excitement infectious. "New Orleans! Isn't that Great!"

I can hear a long stream of helpless stammering on the other end. "What? I thought you were in Northern California on your way home! Girl! You gotta come home!"

"But, Pop, listen to that music!"

His protests are washed out by the sounds as I hold the phone out like a lighter at a rock concert.

As I bring the receiver back to my ear, I can hear that the sneeze of excitement I blew at him hasn't given him even a sniffle of joy. I've been lying to him, telling him I've been traveling around all summer in a hippie van with a girl named Flower. He wasn't ready to hear that his fifteen-year-old daughter has been hitching around the country with her nineteen-year-old boyfriend. It's not like this is the 60's. It's 1999 and I don't see other kids out here thumbing around.

I end the call abruptly as his questions start to rise. You and I check out the situation. The summer is ending and I know it's time for me to head back to Washington. You're not coming with me. The long gray winters and dim people stifle your artistry.

Our days are numbered by Subway stamps now. Every twelve stamps gives us one foot-long sandwich. We stole enough stamps to award us each one foot-long a day for a week. Six inches for lunch. Six for dinner.

Now that we've run out of Subway stamps, we're not saying anything about it, but I know we're both wondering how we're going to eat. We're out of money and out of options. As we wander back to the motel, I see a statue with his arm outstretched. There is a brown bag hung from his bronze fingers. An inner voice tells me to go have a look. I go to the statue and look inside and it is overflowing with bagels and pastries. I nearly fall to the ground with joy. We had no idea how we were going to eat. We eagerly bite into fancy Danishes and bubble over with laughter.

It is profound how we've been provided for. Truckers have bought us hotel rooms when we had nowhere else to sleep. People have given us money even though we weren't asking for it. Drivers have taken us miles out of their way so we could get to where we wanted to go. I trust now that we'll never go hungry. The universe wants to give.

It feels like we're being wrapped up by the world. I feel the tension of the life we left behind like a distant foghorn. Out here, we've been called to stretch ourselves beyond what we were taught and learn what each new moment is bringing. We've had to be in tune with which rides to take and which to turn away. The fate of where we end up has been up to whoever decides to stop. You and I have had to be seamlessly woven together. Working as one unit, using a language beyond words. With a glance, we've had to know what the other is thinking and feeling. Relying on a wisdom deeper than what our minds can drum up.

How do we say goodbye to a love like this? You are more than my first love. More than a travel companion. You are sewn *into the very fabric of my being.*

Back at the roach infested motel, somehow we seem to know that this is our last shower together. As we wash each other's bodies, I ask you to sing me the song you sang the first night I spent with you. As you sing, you look down at me, and cradle my face in your hands. The sweetness of your voice, shaky with emotion.

"And I see you there with the rose in your teeth. One more thin gypsy thief."

Your tears fall into my eyes, blend with my own tears and are washed down our bare bodies. You interrupt the melodies to press your lips to mine. Each time our lips meet, more tears fall. Intuitively we know this is the end of us. I taste you all the way into my belly, a flavor that will never leave me.

The last song goodbye,

Kamala

When we live our lives intuitively, we open to deeply connect with ourselves, others, and the world around us. Exercising our intuitive awareness brings us into the moment and invites us to engage with the aliveness and gifts of life. Heightening intuitive awareness, to perceive beyond the straight lines of life, is simply a matter of fine-tuning ordinary senses to expand beyond them. Like a wine connoisseur with taste buds that can discern the weather conditions grapes endured, you too can heighten your ability to see, hear, feel, taste, and smell subtle energy.

Looking through a mundane lens of perception to see only the tangible physical aspects of our world, we miss the richness of our existence. It is through the ordinary that we can develop something extraordinary. Our basic functions of seeing, hearing, feeling, tasting, and smelling are gateways to tap into the more subtle energetic realms of which we are a part.

If we look at the physical world as if we are seeing all there is to see, we stop seeing what's underneath. When we pay attention to what we are sensing, and slow down enough to hear the subtleties, we make space to hear our intuition.

Being present to our senses makes them more acute, and, with conscious intent, we can develop a heightened experience of what is "normal." For example, you see someone on the street who you think you know. You look for visual cues to try to identify the person. You may scan for body structure, hair color, and posture. Once you find an answer you are satisfied with, like, "Oh, that's Joe," then, you stop scanning for information. But if you keep looking, keep scanning, you might notice something you hadn't noticed before. Perhaps Joe is holding the exact answers you've been seeking. Whenever you are trying to see something and you get an adequate answer, keep using your eyes to try and see more. When we approach people with curiosity and inquiry, it opens pathways for both intuition and intimacy to flourish.

Push your senses beyond the threshold of satisfaction and challenge yourself to seek more. At first you may not notice anything different, but remember, it's subtle. Don't let your brain try to rationalize what you're experiencing.

Roadmap to Intimacy—Seven Playful Ways to Practice Enhancing Intuition

1. The next time you see something out of the corner of your eye, rather than disregard it as the mind playing tricks, let your attention follow it.

2. The next time you are trying to decipher what spices have been used in the dinner you're eating, see if you can detect the subtle flavors of how the cook was feeling when preparing the meal.

3. Take moments to look at your current landscape. Can you see, feel, hear anything that, perhaps, you hadn't noticed before? Look deeper. Listen more attentively. Let smells tickle your nose hairs.

4. We are not collectively taught about life outside the box, so listen to your first response. Your first impulse is your body wisdom speaking before the mind can butt in. Experiment with following your first impulse. Notice what happens when you do.

5. Slow down. Rather than rushing ahead and doing what you think you should be doing, spend time only taking actions that are both relaxing and inspiring. When you slow down, there are more opportunities to hear the subtleties of your natural impulses.

6. Follow your gut impulse. Whenever you get a feeling in your stomach that you need to do something, do it. Don't second guess yourself.

7. Practice walking through your day as though everyone you interact with has the wisdom you've been seeking. As though each person is divine and holy. Notice how much closeness is generated when you move through the world like this.

Pushing the Edge

Dear Easton,

Sleeping on church property somewhat worked for us before, so we meander over to the large brick building. The door is propped open, and there is a light on. I peek in and can hear people talking down the hall. I silently slip in through the door and motion you to follow. We dart down a hall in the opposite direction of the voices and climb some stairs. There are many classrooms, and I push open a door to a storage room. We lay our sleeping bags onto the linoleum, plug in an old fan, grab some bottles of juice from a fridge, strip our clothes, and lay down for the night. It's steamy hot, and the fan tickling our bare skin is the only relief from the thick humid air.

Things would have been different if we had known it was our last night together. Perhaps we would have stayed awake all night gazing into one another, or said all the things our hearts felt, or shared our tears through our kisses. We don't know though. We make love, as blissfully as we always do, on the cooled linoleum of the house of god, and fall peacefully asleep in one another's arms.

Now it's morning. We dodge the voices in the church

and walk across the street to the house of waffles. We tote our heavy, well-worn bags in through the sticky diner doors. The southerners, who seem to live at the tables they're sitting at, all stop to glare at us as we walk in. I take a slight note of my messy hair. My flowery tank top and patchwork shorts expose my lawn of unshaven armpits and legs. Your hair in a greasy mohawk, matching your faded and torn t-shirt.

I think they're glaring because, somehow, they know we just desecrated their church and played Adam and Eve where their kids learn about sin. The unfriendly waitress serves us heaping plates through nicotine clouds. We mop up the last of our syrup and gravy and step into the already rising Mississippi morning heat. Humidity causes our clothes to cling to us as if we were in a rainstorm.

We make our way back to work on the highway. If we could have peered into our crystal ball, we never would have stepped onto the highway that day. How could we have known that right there on that freeway would mark the end of you and me?

We've spent three months hitching across twenty states. I came out here thinking I was going to learn about the harsh realities of people. Learn what I was always told, that the world is a cruel place filled with people who can't be trusted. Again and again though, that belief has been shattered. Stranger after stranger showed us that people are inherently good. People want to help, they're just waiting for someone to ask. It seemed we'd learn about the evils of man, but instead we learned that it is not man who is corrupt; instead it is the system in which we live.

We slip into a violent haze as we become hypnotized by the zooming cars. We don't normally hitch directly on the highway, but today we are desperate. It seems our desperation overshadows our intuition that we shouldn't be here. My plane out of Little Rock leaves tomorrow, and we still have a great distance to go. The cars flying by send us into some hopeless trance. We try to finger our way to the end of a journey well lived. We sing songs at the top of our lungs. Our voices matching the wails of passing cars. The scratchy tones of Bohemian Rhapsody lift us out of our bodies and we lose our focus of why we're here.

That is how the first car that stops finds us.

Belting, "Just gotta get out, just gotta get out, just gotta get right out of here!"

Off key.

We hardly notice a car pulled over for us. Once we do, our typical elation of a ride instead feels like a punch in the stomach. The flashing blue and red lights seem to disorient us even more. Two police men step out with questions. I assume this will be like our police ride in Roswell, when the cop drove us into the next town with a "have a nice day."

I tell them I have a plane ticket out of Arkansas the next day. You, anti-authority, loudly boast of our extensive hitching travels. They ask us our ages. I lie and say I'm sixteen, and you say nineteen. All of a sudden it's like a movie. My face is pressed against the hood of the car, hands being cuffed behind my back, rights being read.

Like a dog, I'm tossed into the back of the car. I am so confused and disoriented. What's going on? All of a sudden the car's moving. I strain my body around to see you through the back window. You're still standing on the side of the road. Wailing, I kick at the back of the seat as if my blows will magically bust the car apart and set me free. We're speeding away and you're getting smaller. You quickly disappear from my view.

At the station, I am hysterical. My hands and feet are chained to a bench. There are three police officers questioning me.

"Don't people shave their legs in Washington? When's the last time you took a shower?" They scoff at me like some dirty animal.

I am blinded by tears and snot that my chained hands can't wipe away. All I want is to see you again. I try to make them understand how this is our last goodbye. They are going through my pack. They read my journal out loud and laugh at me. I pull against the chains, trying to get it back. I feel so humiliated, so exposed.

I tell them to call my parents. "They know exactly where I am. I am catching a plane out of Little Rock tomorrow. I'll take a bus the rest of the way there."

"What kinda parent would let ya be hitchhiking? You're neva gonna to see yo family again. Yo gonna to end up in foster care. You ain't go'n back to a family like dat."

All three of them take turns taunting and threatening me. I am a wild animal thrashing against my chains. I keep demanding my phone call, but they tell me since I am a minor, I don't have any rights. They take me outside to go through my backpack. The empty Tupperware clinks against the ground. Just a short time earlier it was filled with drugs, and I am so relieved that I have sold, smoked, and eaten the last of them.

As we walk back inside, I see you out the window. You're walking away from the station. I rush over and start banging on the glass with my cuffed hands. I yell your name at the top of my lungs and you turn around and see me. You slowly approach the window as if it's electric. I yell at the officers to let me see you, but they tell me they refused you and threatened to arrest you since I'm a minor and you're not.

We look helplessly into one another.

You press your hand to the window and I lift mine to meet you. Our hands touch with the glass between us. Yours free, mine chained.

We both mouth, "I love you," as tears tumble from our eyes. As they pull me from the window and chain me to the bench again, you abruptly turn and walk away as if it's too painful to watch.

You dissolve into the humidity like a mirage,

Kamala

Intimacy can be terrifying.

There is a reason for the disparity of intimacy in our culture. Being intimate calls us to be incredibly authentic and honest and vulnerable in real time. When we open to others, we take a risk. We risk being rejected or hurt or shamed or shot down or left. So how do we manage the potential pain we're opening ourselves to when we start engaging intimately with others?

It's important to be able to regulate what's in our comfort zone, what's pushing past our comfort zone, and what is pushing us completely over the edge. If you want to open yourself to another and intimately engage and feel deep levels of connection, you have to move out of your comfort zone. Your comfort zone is where you're on autopilot. Your comfort zone keeps you on the couch watching movies. Your comfort zone keeps you repeating the same old patterns. And that's okay. It's perfectly alright for you to hang out in your comfort zone as much as you want to be there.

When you're ready to feel a deeper connection to yourself and others, you need to be willing to move out of your comfort zone and push your edge. When you're pushing your edge, you're opening yourself to learning and growing and moving deeper into intimacy.

Sometimes you can push your edge too far and you'll fall over. Going over your edge doesn't help you to break patterns, or experience more intimacy. The space between pushing your edge and going over your edge can be a fine line. It takes knowing yourself and continually practicing being present with yourself so you bump up against your edge without falling over.

If we push ourselves too far too fast, we risk hurting ourselves.

> How do we know if we are hanging out in our comfort zone and not growing?

> How do we know if we're pushing the edge of our comfort zone and creating space for intimacy and connection?

> How do we know if we're about to fall over our edge, and into a place of perpetuating tension?

You know you're in your comfort zone when:

- → You're not aware of what your body is doing
- → You're not present
- → You're going through the motions
- → You seem like you could be on autopilot
- → You reach for media—your phone, a movie, food, sugar, alcohol, drugs, sex in order to feel better

You know you're pushing your edge and moving toward deeper connection with yourself and others when:

→ You are present in the moment
→ You're aware of what sensations you're feeling in your body
→ You're aware of your breath
→ You're breathing deeply
→ You're able to relax your body
→ You're not making up stories
→ You're curious about what is happening within you and in the world around you
→ You're able to openly share about what is happening for you in the moment

You know you're going over your edge and risking re-traumatizing yourself when:

→ Your body is tense
→ You're constricting your breath
→ You can't focus
→ You feel the need to run away
→ You feel like fighting, arguing or attacking the person in front of you
→ You feel like shutting down and pulling away
→ You feel numb or overwhelmed

The trick to knowing where you stand is to mindfully track what is happening in your own body. Your breath and your body are your barometers for intimacy. If you're not aware of what is happening in your own body, you're chilling out in your disconnected comfort zone. There isn't anything inherently wrong with that, but it's helpful to be aware of where you stand.

When your breath starts to speed up and get shallow and your body becomes tense or numb, you know you've pushed yourself too far and you need to ease up on the throttle. When you've pushed yourself too far, this is when arguments happen. This is when we start to create stories about why either ourselves or our partners are not meeting our needs. But when the porridge is just right, when we're pushing our edge just enough, we can fully enjoy the feast of deep connection to ourselves and others, as well as profound states of love.

When you push yourself too far too fast, you're not doing anyone a favor. Intimacy and connection require incredible patience, mindfulness, and acceptance of yourself. Finding the intimacy sweet spot isn't complicated, but it takes constant practice and consideration. Begin by finding an awareness of your body. Turn the dial of your intimacy barometer by consciously relaxing your body and deepening your breath.

We can change our view of the world and our perception of our partners simply by breathing deeper. When we perceive any kind of danger, the first thing we do is hold our breath. Our nervous system goes on alert and we're not able to see the truth of what is happening in the moment. We start to think the person in front of us is attacking us or withdrawing their love.

Your body is a library for everything that has ever happened to it. Much like a tree shaped by wind, your body is shaped by the pains and pleasures it has experienced. When we try to override any part of ourselves, the body will speak up. For instance, if we use sex to try and fill a void or to feel better, then we might be overriding what we are experiencing emotionally.

The body constantly sends us messages. What may feel good in one moment, may not feel good in the next. What may be the key to get you off one day, may not be what your body needs the next. I invite you to pay attention to your ever-changing ever-present needs. Each time you pay attention to a need, you actually build a sense of safety and trust, which is essential for intimacy. It may be your own need or the need of your partner.

When you approach with curiosity and wanting to know what each present moment desire is, you create space for opening and building trust. And the more there is presence, the more all of you can open. Presence is being with the experience moment by moment. It means every time something painful comes up, that we don't want to experience, we stay with it. We feel it in our own bodies and we let it go. To accomplish this openness, we must continually come back to awareness, and be gentle with ourselves when we forget.

Each time we feel hurt and betrayed by another, walls come up. These walls can be paper thin and hardly noticeable or they can be barbed. We think we're doing ourselves a favor.

We say, "I need these walls to protect myself," and we stay buried behind the walls, fermenting in our own pain.

But the walls don't take the pain away. The walls cause the pain. We get angry and wonder how the other could have hurt us. We blame and we shut off until there is no place for love to flow. It hurts to stop the flow of love.

There are few things as painful as shutting off your heart. We point fingers and say, "See what you made me do! Because of you, I was forced to shut off my heart and now I am suffering. I will punish you by not loving you. I will punish you by inflicting the greatest pain onto myself... shutting off my heart."

Additionally, we will build even more walls of protection and say, "See! I knew it. This always happens to me. I open myself up and people hurt me. I'm not going to open myself up anymore."

Think about all the different aspects of human beings as circles. Every time we experience pain or trauma a circle is broken. If we are not present with the pain we are experiencing and give ourselves the love we need in that moment, the circle stays broken. Often times, we override the experience or try to push it away because we're afraid of the pain.

All those broken circles get buried in the body, waiting to be reconnected.

When we get into painful situations, broken circles start bubbling to the surface, desperate to be reconnected. In order for these circuits of ourselves to become whole again, we often seek external circumstance (lovers, drugs, media) to fill in the gaps. We set other people up to fail by subconsciously begging them to offer the missing element of love that will make us whole again. Our expectations are too unreasonable because only you have the keys to fill that emptiness. People fail, and our circles of self become even more fragmented. No one and nothing can complete the circuit of us as human beings except for our own presence and lovingly holding those hurting parts.

People hurt others because they are hurting. When we don't honor ourselves, we can't honor others. I hear people wondering how others could commit such horrendous crimes like murder and rape. When people feel numb or are hurting inside, there are many things people would do to stop feeling that pain. We are all capable of terrible things. Perhaps you've cheated or lied to your partner, but that does not make you a bad person.

People don't open to love through abuse, locking them away, or punishment. That only teaches people to disconnect and become numb. If we want to share and bring more peace to this world, we need to enhance our basic skills of intimacy.

When we treat ourselves and one another with love, honor, care and respect, then there is no room for feeling victimized. There is no room for pain to take over. If we were taught basic skills of intimacy, emotional honesty, and expressing love, then this world would be a much different place. If people knew how to meet their own needs and extend a hand to others, love would grow within.

Sometimes we're faced with more than we feel we can deal with. Sometimes the pain of a situation becomes so overwhelming that we lose contact with ourselves. Sometimes we check out or try to drown out the pain of what we're experiencing. There are so many brilliant ways that we try to cope with stress, trauma, and pain. One of the most common is to become disconnected from our bodies.

Why would we stay in our bodies when that is where the pain is? If we shut out the body, we also shut out pleasure, passion, and connecting deeply with another. It is in the body where we come to life and are able to merge who we are with who we want to be. It is coming back to the present moment that makes overcoming hardship possible.

The problem with burying the broken circles of self behind walls is that they don't go away. They linger below the surface, dictate our behaviors, and skew how we see the world. Walling yourself off and shutting down is the worst way to protect yourself. All that does is bury those fragmented parts of ourselves deeper. Trauma and ignored pain doesn't just go away. When not addressed, trauma and pain can get buried in the body, waiting dormant to trigger a fight, flight, or freeze response. If we give ourselves what we need, help to reconnect the circles, we become whole and integrated people.

How do we reconnect the circuits and heal the parts of ourselves that aren't flowing and functioning at full capacity?

The answer is in presence. We don't reach outside ourselves for someone else to rescue us. We don't numb out and try to distract ourselves from the pain. Instead we cradle it. We feel it in our own beautiful bodies. We notice what sensations and emotions are arising and we say, "Welcome." We give ourselves, moment by moment, the love that we need, the attention we've always longed for, while honoring where we are in our journey.

Roadmap to Intimacy—Pushing Your Edge

In a comfortable and safe space, allow yourself to find stillness.

1. Guide your breath to be as rhythmic and slow as crashing waves. Place one hand on your belly and one on your heart. Relax into the ease of being held.

2. Gently bring a situation to mind that feels painful.

3. Monitor your breath. Keep breathing deeply. Deep breathing sends a signal to the body that it is safe.

4. Find a location where you can mentally place the situation and still maintain a feeling of safety. It may be in the corner of the room. It may be all the way on the moon.

5. As you breathe in, see if you can inch the situation closer to you while remaining relaxed. Allow it to come as close as it can without creating any tension in you. You're in control.

6. The key is to keep your breath deep in your belly. When your belly stops moving, you know you're moving into a risk zone and it's time to move the situation farther away. As you exhale, allow the situation to return to where it feels best for you.

7. Keep one hand on your heart to let you know you're safe, and one hand on your belly to encourage you to breathe deeply. Repeat for 5-10 minutes.

Summary & Quotes to Share

As we deepen our breath and enhance our awareness of our bodies, we can relax more into the moment, feel
safer, and trust others and ourselves more fully. By paying
attention to the subtle aspects of our senses, we learn the
language of what our bodies need. In turn, we trust our
intuition more fully.

Opening to Pleasure

❖ Intimacy invites us into deep connection to others
and ourselves.

❖ When we are intimately engaged with life, everything we experience is pleasurable.

❖ Trust is essential to experiencing increased levels of
pleasure.

Being Present to Who Someone Is

❖ In order to see a situation or person for what it is, we
need to gain perspective by taking a step back.

❖ By dropping our walls of fear-based protection, we
have the opportunity to be surprised by others.

❖ Being present allows us to walk through our lives
discovering the love that is present in every moment.

Fully Trusting Yourself—Breathe

❧ Deepening our breath can bring us back into our bodies, and help us dissolve untrue stories we're making up.

❧ Being in our body helps us to know what we do and do not want, and strengthens our self-trust.

❧ If we want our nervous system to calm into a state of openness and connection, we deepen our breath.

We Need Each Other

❧ The people we love hold the keys to the deepest parts of us. We need others to access more of who we are.

❧ Intimacy invites us to burn through the obstacles that hold us back from expressing.

❧ Each person offers a reflection of what is alive and waiting to be awakened within us.

Drinking in What Each Moment Offers

❧ Our senses can connect us with our bodies and bring us into the moment.

❧ Our senses are messengers from the subconscious aspects of ourselves.

❧ When we stay curious about what we sensing, we can access the messages that our bodies are trying to tell us.

Intuitive Living

❖ When we live our lives intuitively, we open to deeply connect with ourselves, others, and the world around us.

❖ Through paying attention to what we are sensing, and slowing down enough, we make space to hear our intuition.

❖ When we approach people with curiosity, it opens pathways for both intuition and intimacy to flourish.

Letting Go of Pain

❖ Our comfort zone is where we're on autopilot and not growing.

❖ When we're ready for deeper connection, we need to be willing to move out of our comfort zone and push our edges.

❖ It's important to identify what's in our comfort zone, what's helping us grow, and what's pushing us over the edge.

❖ If we push ourselves over our edges, we risk hurting ourselves.

✉ Share on Facebook and Tweet @KamalaChambers

TWO

JEDIAH
Busting Out of Old Patterns

After experiencing the freedom and love I had with Easton, moving back to the city and mundane living was heartbreaking. I coped with the loss of freedom through addictions to drugs, alcohol and a new man... Jediah.

Over the course of 4 years, I struggled to break free from my addictions and get away from Jediah once and for all. In multiple attempts to break out of my old patterns, I left him behind and went on extensive travels, but my continual longing for him kept me coming back.

I hitchhiked to Alaska and around nine countries in Europe. Through my travels, I learned curiosity is essential for intimacy, listening to body language is key to communication, and trying new things is fundamental to growth.

It wasn't until I met an unlikely character that I experienced the awakening I needed to end my relationship with

Jediah once and for all. Through these letters, lessons and exercises, I invite you to break out of your own patterns that have been holding you back from living and loving at your fullest potential.

Busting Out of Old Patterns

Dear Jediah,

We're not meant to be together and we both know it. You find me so lonely, and desperate to feel freedom again, that I'm easy to mold. For our first months together, we're drunk and stoned on wine and weed and whatever illicit substances we can scrounge up.

I wash out my days with malt liquor. All my questions are asked to screw tops, as if answers lay at the bottom of the bottle. The questions are forgotten by the time I take the last swig though.

After the magic I've discovered on the road, being trapped in the city is a spiral downward. Down like the alcohol flowing into my mouth, like rain down a gutter. The tenderness in my heart blooms on my sixteenth birthday and then slowly wilts into this bottomless chasm. The word "tender" mutates; it once meant gentle and loving, and now I tender my wages for weed. My bruised, tender heart falls like an overripe plum in the pit of my belly. The only comfort? Writing love letters I will not send and tickling well-worn memories that will never be shared with you.

You and I wander the woods and streets at all hours. In the woods, we jump down steep, sandy cliffs, muddy from the recent rains. Downwards until we reach the water's edge. Washing the dirt from my hands in the brittle coldness of the Puget Sound, for a moment I feel alive. We walk the length of the beach toward an inevitable setting sun. You never let silence hang for long before you fill up the space with another monologue. I stay quiet as grief. We play like that until the colors fade and a sliver moon shines through the trees.

In the streets, we memorize cracked sidewalks, and follow lines of grass struggling through the pavement as if we're that grass fighting to thrive in a land of concrete. The season changes, and the trees lose their leaves like I lose my clarity. Full of doubt my mind races for answers, I turn toward the clouds only to find more questions.

"Take me away from here," I beg to you while you're sleeping. You take a deep breath and roll away from me. I settle back to dream with wide-open eyes. All I want is distance from the emptiness.

I tell you everything about me except what really matters, the parts of me that are with Easton. He is the part of me that I'll never let you close enough to see. All you know of me is my pain, and it's pulled you to me like a tractor beam. Together, we happily sip our wine of sorrow and fill our days with smoke signals. But my nights are for him. My dreams are wild horses pulling me on their wings. All night long my dreams make love to me. Easton and I merge on levels you'll never understand. And each morning, I am shocked to find you here, confused by your awkward touch and dim eyes. You're like the bad taste on my tongue. I'm back here in this cold basement next to you instead of out on the road with him.

I feel so ashamed that you have stained me. My tongue thick with the lies of our kisses. I can't keep lying. Being with you betrays everything I opened with Easton. I let you touch my body and your fingers scorch me. I leave my body here for you to cum in while my heart and thoughts wander and weave with him. The only relief is the miniature orgasms that follow.

My thumbs grow itchy. They can only be scratched by the rough hand of the highway. I stretch out the neck of my thumb to see if its powers still hold. These thumbs were great once. They wielded the power of pulling a stranger toward me and letting me into their world. I've been hitching bottles these days. Flagging down the cheapest wines and whiskies hailing beers and booze as if they'll fling me from this place.

Now, they drum the edge of empty glasses and counterbalance tipping bottles. There is only so far riding bottles can take me.

The only way to break free from you is to do something different. I'm taking off. I'm crawling out from this drug haze we've been in for months and hitting the road. Please, do us both a favor and don't wait for me. All you do is remind me of what I've lost and what I threw away. You're like a drug. You have your grip on me. I need you, and I despise you for it.

Quitting you cold turkey and hitting the road,

Kamala

The more we repeat a pattern, the deeper we dig ourselves into a groove. If you walk the same route every day through the forest, you'll eventually create a path. If you think the same thoughts, repeat the same feelings, and continue the same behaviors in your relationships, you'll eventually dig a groove until that groove becomes a rut. The more you repeat those patterns, the harder it will be to break out of them.

One of the best ways to break out of old patterns is to do something different. This means whatever your default behavior is, do the opposite. If you keep doing the same thing the way you've always done it, you set yourself up for living on autopilot. Have you ever driven someplace you've been to a hundred times before and don't remember driving there? It's easy to go through our days and relationships stuck on repeat, not fully tapped into the presence of what is here.

Relaxation holds the key to fully facing these ruts. When we approach our issues from a state of relaxation, we break the walls of the rut we've dug for ourselves. Relaxation allows us to sit outside our unhealthy patterns. When we relax, it's easier to break patterns because we're not carrying the tension of the stories around in our bodies. From a state of relaxation we can make a choice of whether we want to constrict around our stories again or let them move out.

From a relaxed space, we can pay attention to our patterns and access the messages they are offering. We can move out of any self-loathing that we have about our cravings. We can even meet our cravings with gratitude for the messages they are providing. Patterns, cravings and even addictions aren't bad. Cravings and addictive tendencies are just messages from ourselves telling us that we have deeper needs. These are opportunities to listen to ourselves, see that we have unmet needs, and fulfill those needs.

Trying new things can also be a powerful way to fulfill our own unmet needs, whether they are a product of ourselves, or our relationships. Some of the happiest couples, who have been together the longest, practice spontaneity. They do things that are new and exciting. They don't get caught in ruts because they keep doing things that are different. If you want to break out of the cycles of arguing, continually drawing in "bad" relationships, or having a mediocre sex life, you have to be willing to keep trying new things and stepping out of what is familiar. If you keep doing the same thing, no matter how good it feels, it will eventually lose its spark.

Many times in relationships we only go for what is predictable. Is there something you keep repeating sexually because it's what you've found works? I invite you to be an explorer. I invite you to not be on autopilot with your sexual interactions. You have to be willing to give up what you think you need to do in order to experience all new levels of pleasure and passion. No matter how good it is now, trust me, it can always be better.

When we approach sex and intimacy with curiosity, it becomes fun. We keep discovering what is here and asking to be uncovered. When we don't make up our minds about things and meet the world with curiosity in every moment, we get to meet each moment with true presence. When we move into intimacy as an explorer, we keep unfolding what's new and present. When we are curiously engaged with the sensations of the moment, we create more space for intimacy, love, and pleasure.

Feeling pleasure is just a by-product of physical intimacy. The more you can awaken the sensations in your body, the more access you have to yourself and the more alive you feel. If we take superb care of our bodies, hearts, minds, and emotions, we have way more access to who we are and what gifts we have to share with others.

Going straight for sexual sensation is like going straight for cake. Intimacy on the other hand is like planting a garden, harvesting the veggies, and cooking a deeply nourishing delicious meal. Yes, it takes more time, but the journey can offer lasting fulfillment. Just having the cake of sex, you stuff it all in and then crash. If you just eat cake for dinner, chances are you're not going to feel as good as you would if you prepared a healthy home cooked meal.

The cake of sex is more than a metaphor. The way we feed our bodies directly affects how we feel. If we feel crappy, there is a good chance we're not going to feel like engaging intimately. Sometimes people make arguments about not eating healthy food and live off of junk food. They say they don't care if they die young. However, eating healthy, nourishing food and making love with full presence is about feeling as alive and vibrant as we can. When we eat better, we feel better. When we slow down sexually, we feel more.

The foods you eat directly affect your sex life. Foods that are good for the heart are also good for getting the penis and clitoris pumping. Consuming foods that are high in arginine and/or omega-3 can help get your circulation going. To name a few, try salmon, green vegetables, and seeds.

Breaking eating habits can be a powerful way to experience deeper intimacy. Eating "romantic" foods can kill the mood. Wine may numb your senses. The sugar in cake could make you tense. Pasta, bread, and cheese might leave you feeling sleepy and bloated. Pay attention to what you eat before you make love and the quality of the experience. Look for correlations between the foods you eat, your mood, and your sex life.

Invite your partner to help break eating patterns with you. Make food itself sexy. Spend time cooking with your partner, and when you do, treat your kitchen like an extension of your bedroom. Take your time and experiment with new flavors. Appreciate the texture, smell, and sensation of enjoying food with your partner.

Roadmap to Intimacy—Breaking Patterns

1. Either write about or share with a partner a pattern you keep repeating. Go through the motions of this pattern in your mind. How does it feel in your body to repeat this pattern? What emotions are linked to this pattern? How do you feel?

2. There is a reason you keep repeating this pattern. What does this pattern offer you? What is pleasurable and enjoyable about this pattern? What need does it fill?

3. Now that you've identified the need that this pattern fulfills, what are some other alternatives to meeting that need? Exercising, eating a healthier, taking some time alone…whatever it might be, really consider what else you can do as an alternative to meet that need.

4. Now, notice whenever you're starting to repeat that pattern. Notice the familiar body sensations and emotions, and let those be your indicators that you're repeating the pattern. Ask yourself, "What can I do instead right now?" And make the choice to do something different.

Longing

Dear Jediah,

After dipping down to the crystal pools and red rocks of Sedona and Zion, I'm under the vast skies of Montana now. My oldest brother Marcus and I are preparing our thumbs to hitch across Canada to Alaska. We've been on the road a few months, and I'm still detoxing you. You're like a claw in my belly, slowly and methodically scratching at my insides. I cradle my hitching thumb as though it's the only thing that will carry me far enough away from you.

As we climb through canyons, wander through thick forests, and watch the blur of passing landscape, I try to forget you. You murder my daydreams and drench me in bloody yearning. The only thing more powerful than longing for you is my longing not to yearn for you.

Jediah, being away from you for these months is strange. I don't think about good times we had. Honestly, I can't recall any. I don't anticipate how good it could feel to be with you. It's like all you are is the feeling of emptiness. In my mind I'm having a love affair with you, but my affair is with longing itself. Longing for you has penetrated me to the core and moves as deeply in me as marrow. You are nothing more now than my own emptiness. I ache for you to be close to me. Like a junkie, I'm hungry for the fix of your touch. You are nothing more than longing now.

Oh sweet Longing, you've always been here for me to claw at my heart and keep me reaching. Your hungry mouth becomes my hungry mouth. I try to feed you Longing, but your belly of emptiness is never full.

Your thirsty eyes are my thirsty eyes. I try to quench your thirst until my face burns with tear rashes and there is an ocean at my feet. Longing, your touchless embrace seems like the only thing I could rely on. And now, Longing, I want to leave you for your brother. I am so sorry, Longing. We've been so intertwined. I want to miss you, Longing, but if you leave, you'll take the ability to miss.

In the heat of my own embrace, I believe I can meet your most incredible brother and fall into the deepest love. He can move deeper into me than bone. His love can transform my DNA.

Thank you for our life together, Longing. But I want to get married to your brother, Fulfillment. I'm on the hunt for Fulfillment. He has to be out here somewhere.

Before we cross the border, we spend a week in the dust at this year's Peace Gathering. I find nostalgia and feel like I've gotten all I can from these drug-drenched "peace" parties in the woods. Marcus and I walk across the border with minimal hassle from the Canadians.

We travel well together. Most of our communication is telepathic, so there is little need for spoken words. We head into Banff National Park and spend days overpowered by waterfalls and wildlife. We blaze on through tiny towns. When it gets too dark to hitch, we wander into the forest and make camp. Our rides are easy to come by and vary between lone truckers to curious tourists to men on their way to work.

We follow the road as far as we can, until we dead-end at the Pacific Ocean, in Prince Rupert. My brothers Lee and Aden meet us here. They come up by bus and we all board a boat to Alaska. Maybe the chill of Alaska will purge out the last of you, and my mind will be free to roam without you weighing me down.

Alaska is just as dramatic with wildlife, mountains, thick trees, and bear warnings as we imagined it to be. As soon as we enter Alaska, though, we step into a raincloud that never moves. Days of sopping shoes make us unsettled. We keep looking over our shoulders for Noah's ark. Something about being wet and cold makes me crave you more, as if you're the hot chocolate in *the snow lodge.*

My three brothers and I arrive at the end of the road to the gaping mouth of the ancient ice of the Mendenhall Glacier. As we peer into the three thousand year old melting monolith, it's as if we're reaching a hand through time. It's a piercing blue that is so violent, it puts the shocking blue of our four sets of eyes to shame. There is something so overpowering about this glacier that makes us uneasy. It reminds us of our smallness. The discomfort of beauty seeps through our clothes like the rain does, and we shiver in its cold presence.

It all becomes just too much for us. The four of us begin to argue. I'm not even sure what we're all so angry about. It's as if we have to do something to break apart the feelings this all-knowing ice is drawing out of us. The glacier evokes an inescapable loneliness. And we are all stirred with longing to the core for the ones we left behind. I am overwhelmed with needing you right now.

To try and calm us, Marcus heats up refried beans from a can. He turns the camp stove on full blast, as if he can melt the tension the glassy ice is cutting into us. A horrific smell rises as aluminum and beans burn together. And with the smell, comes more yelling. I break away from my brothers and go to the edge of the glacier and cry. I cry for its awesome beauty and for the loneliness of months on the road. Overtaken by my insignificance at the feet of this boulder of water, I cry because I want you with a yearning so deep my bones ache. Despite the months on the road I've worked to cleanse you out of my system, I won't be able to help but go back to you. I thought out here, in the wilds, I would be filled by unmistakable peace. But instead it seems my longing for you has only intensified. Wet, shivering, post-argument, lonely, too far from home, sleep deprived from bears shuffling outside our tent, but the absolute worst part is I know I'm going back to you.

A hand lands on my shoulder, and although I want to hide my tears, I look up with wet eyes to see my brother Lee peering into me as deeply as the glacier's blue-eyed glare.

"Let's go home," is all he says.

Devastated and delighted to know
I'm coming home to you,

Kamala

Longing can create an aching within that causes us to crave someone the same way we crave a drug. Longing gives us something to focus on. It gives us something to reach for. We can have the same relationship with fulfillment as we do with longing. We can shift how much we long for someone, just by shifting our relationship with longing itself. We can have a relationship to a feeling as much as we have a relationship to a person. It is easy to get addicted to feeling a certain way. The more we feel that way, the more we crave feeling that way. If we eat junk food every day, we're going to crave junk food. If feeling longing is common for us, we're going to seek that feeling out.

Sometimes when we're craving another, it seems like they are the only thing that will make the inner aching stop. Longing for another is an opportunity to shift focus from what we desire to what we already have.

Often times it seems just seeing someone or having sex with them is what we need to feel better. Sex is not a way to satisfy an unmet need or longing. Making love enhances what is already here. If you feel empty inside before you make love, chances are you're going to end up feeling even emptier once it's over. When you feel deeply fulfilled before you make love, the well of your heart will overflow.

Roadmap to Intimacy—Break Free from Longing

1. Think about someone you long to be near. Notice what craving them feels like in your body. Notice what longing for them feels like in your belly. Rather than staying focused on this person, focus on the sensations of what it's like to miss this person.

2. Set those sensations aside. Now, place one hand on your belly and one hand on your heart. Breathe deeply into your belly. Notice what it's like to be held. Notice what it's like to have this undivided attention being offered to you. As if your own hands could give you everything you need. Imagine what it would be like to be completely fulfilled in this moment. Take some deep breaths into the sensation of fulfillment. Notice what it's like to be settled into yourself.

3. Again, think about the person you long for. Keep one hand on your belly and one on your heart. Keep breathing deeply. Imagine that you are completely fulfilled in this moment, even if this person is not here.

4. Whenever you start miss this person, repeat this practice. Whenever you start to miss or long for them, hold yourself, breathe with yourself and focus on your fulfillment rather than your longing for them. Focus on all the things you have right now in this moment.

Curiosity is Key

Dear Jediah,

Even though I knew better, I came back to you for another nine months. You're a charmer in all the right ways. You know exactly what to say. You're like a leech determined to suck all you can from me. Everything I do, I do for freedom. And yet when I'm with you, I feel like a caged bird, and you're trying to clip my wings.

I'm leaving you yet again. Despite you and weed both stealing my money and weighing me down, I've finished two years of high school this winter and earned enough cash to get out.

I'm on a plane to London. Out the oval window, I watch the quilted land and veins of cracked earth. The story of the world below changes as we cross farmland, desert plateaus, and eventually a seemingly endless expanse of unbroken waters. Getting a bird's view on the world, the confinement of being with you seems small. A curiosity for what lay ahead is waking up in me. Somewhere along the way with you, I forgot how to see the world with fresh eyes.

I feel closer to the miniature version on the landscape below than I feel to you. We've lost sight of each other. Somewhere along the way, I stop being curious about you. From this vantage view, it's easy to remember how important it is to take a step back and get a fresh perspective. Although I'm above the world right now, I somehow feel more a part of it.

Don't wait for me. I know you said you would. My heart aches when I see your pain-stricken face in my mind. It's so hard to pry myself from your talons. I feel like a criminal, robbing you of your prey. I don't even feel like I know you though, and I don't care to. Although we've been playing this game of tug-a-war for two years, we've never looked beyond the drug of each other.

We're all out of eagerness for one another,

Kamala

Thinking we know all we need to know about another is a serious poison to love. The moment we stop seeking and being curious is the moment we stop being present with who someone truly is.

To curiously engage with the world is to experience everything new as if it's the first time. Life is full of first times. As soon as you have one, paradoxically it's your last. Therefore, every choice we make is the most insignificant and significant decision of our lives. When we come at life as an explorer, we continually discover what life is offering us in every moment.

If we stay open and curious about what each moment is bringing, we can dissolve our fears around being hurt by others. Intimacy is happening right here and now. It is not living in the past or trying to dash us into what could happen. What awakens us to intimacy is what is alive in this moment. What guides us into each moment is the desire to discover.

Love and sex are also a process of discovery. Sex is expansive when we treat it as though it is our first time uncovering, moment-by-moment, what feels good, what makes us stir inside, what beckons the other into love. Intimacy is created through being curious about what each moment is bringing.

The aliveness, and the ever-unfolding mystery of sex, can become buried in the mundane. It is a much different experience if your sexual relationship becomes robotic and repetitive. Thinking we know all there is to know about ourselves, the other, or the moment is detrimental to intimacy and living life to the fullest. Each moment is the most terrifying and incredible experience of your life because it is your first and last time to ever experience it.

Roadmap to Intimacy—Five Ways to Meet Life with Curiosity

1. Do something out of character everyday.

2. Whenever you're in front of someone, keep asking yourself, "Who is this beauty before me?"

3. Keep asking yourself, "What else do I have to learn right now?"

4. As often as possible, pretend that this is your first time trying something, no matter how many times you've tried it before. Treat every moment like it's your first, because it is.

5. Approach situations with a whelm of reverence and gratitude for what each encounter and person is bringing you.

Beyond Words

Dear Jediah,

Alone on Schiermonnikoog, an island off the coast of Holland. I am in the only tent in the campground, and haven't seen a person or car or even a house for a week. My days are spent wandering over sand dunes and impossibly flat beaches. Walking across vast expanses of sand, and it seems to take eternity to reach the sea. A week ago, as I checked into the campground, the man behind the counter took my US passport and looked at me with tears in his eyes.

"I so sorry," he said in broken English as he handed my passport back.

I wasn't sure what he was referring to, but found the same shocked concern when I flashed my passport to spend the last of my traveler's checks on seven cans of tuna fish (my only food for the last seven days.)

Today, I called mom and she said last week on September 11, the US was attacked. My quickly fading phone card minutes and her inability to give detail left a jumble of questions in my mind. The point she was trying to make, though, was clear…it's time to come home.

I've been hitchhiking through nine countries for the past three months. My thought was to forego returning home, but it's not often mom gives advice so when she does, I know I should listen.

As I eat the last can of tuna and think about where I've been and where I'm going, I weigh my options. On one hand—I'm on the other side of the world, I'm seventeen, no food, no money, alone, and apparently the US has been attacked or bombed or something.

On the other hand, if I come back, I know you're waiting for me. As soon as you snake charm me with your words, I'll fall back into your grips and maybe never be able to escape. Somehow being starved and alone overseas seems like a better option than coming back to you.

I've gained clarity and strength hitching through countries where the only common language I've had is body language. I've climbed into people's movable worlds and needed to let them know where to take me with nothing more than a tattered map and a monkey form of communication. It's profoundly clear to me now that using words is such a small part of dialogue.

I've been completely incapable of talking to you. Perhaps if I apply what I've learned about body language with you, we can stand a chance. Most of our relationship has been your charm-filled monologues that I silently succumb to. I start to feel *a glimmer of hope that perhaps I can apply what I've learned about speaking with my body and actually get somewhere with you.*

Okay, I'm coming home,

Kamala

.

When you learn to deeply listen to your own body and another person's body, your ability to communicate increases exponentially. Communication extends far beyond words. A person's body and breath will tell you more than words will ever say. Bodies are constantly speaking through posture, minute muscle movement, facial expression, and breathing rate.

When we shift our own bodies to match the sounds, breathing rate, and gestures of others, we can have a deeper understanding of their experience and often they will feel more understood. When we're mirroring another, it's a way to say, "I understand your experience." Rather than just expressing empathy with our words, we can express it with our entire bodies.

We all respond to body language whether we're aware of it or not. Bodies are constantly mirroring each other. When we approach others from a calm and relaxed space, and we're breathing deeply, they won't feel threatened. It's scary for our bodies to have someone approach us who is tense and on high alert. If we want to invite people closer, we need to make sure their bodies feel safe. When we're relaxed, it invites others to relax around us.

When we slow down enough, we can start to translate what the body is saying. When we breathe with awareness in our own bodies, we can start to track the ever so subtle language of how emotions and thoughts affect our bodies. Enhancing our internal awareness can help us translate what other bodies are speaking.

We're taught in childhood what to think and how to feel. Our parents, teachers, and media tell us how we should behave. We're taught to listen to others rather than hear what our own precious bodies are saying. We lose our instinctual awareness. We forget how to listen to other bodies as well. It is in the primalness of our own bodies where we are the most potent. We come alive in our wildness and our domestication unwinds, as we learn to listen to a kinesthetic language words can never access.

Roadmap to Intimacy—Communicate Beyond Words

Communicating with Your Instinctual Awareness

1. Alone, put on some tribal type music with heavy drumming.

2. Imagine what type of mammal you would be if you weren't human.

3. Crouch low to the ground and let the wildness of that animal take over your whole body.

4. Make sounds and movements of that animal for the duration of the whole song.

5. When the song is over, be still and silent and be aware of whatever you're noticing in your body.

6. Breathe deeply and play with how deeply you can relax your body.

Communicating Through Mirroring

1. Sit comfortably with a partner and take slow deep breaths. Notice what is happening in your own body.

2. Gently notice what is happening with your partner's body. Pay attention to their posture, breathing rate, facial expressions, and gestures.

3. Play with ever so slightly mirroring your partner's posture, breath, expressions, and gestures.

4. Now, switch rolls.

5. Share with each other what you noticed.

Communicating with a Lover's Touch

1. You can practice non-verbal communication by placing your lover's hands where you want them.

2. Have your lover place a hand on your hip and then redirect them with your hand to touch where you want to be touched.

3. Give space for your partner to do the same. Make it easy for your lover to redirect you. This builds trust, intimacy, and pleasure.

Try Something New

Dear Jediah,

We pull into 29 Palms on three bad tires and a hunger for free food. Our money is minimal and our appetites big. You and I head for the senior center where we hear they're serving free Thanksgiving dinner.

We sit gorging ourselves on dehydrated potatoes and heaps of turkey swimming in gravy. With half full mouths, we talk about the possibility of getting jobs here. Our well-beaten car isn't going to make it much farther, and back in Washington, you saw Joshua Tree, CA on a map and felt it might be a good place to hide a while.

We throw around a few vague questions about how employers can contact us, since these are the days before every man, woman, and child owns a cell phone. I look up from my cranberries as if to scan the room for answers. My eyes fall on a woman standing on the other side of the room. She jumps and moves toward us as soon as we make eye contact. She quickly floats across the room as if she knows she has the answers to our freshly forming questions.

"What do you guys need?" her friendly voice like an angel answering a prayer.

"We were just thinking about getting jobs and were wondering if there is some kind of local phone service here where we can receive calls."

She doesn't even miss a beat, "you can use my phone."

A little stunned, I explain further, "We're planning on camping out in the park."

"Well as a matter of fact, we have some property behind our house that you can camp on. It butts right up to the park."

After months of living in a tent with our desert angel, it's time we move into our own place. For an outrageously expensive $300 we get a lopsided shack that looks like it was randomly dropped out in the middle of the desert. It's all dust and sky out here.

We're miles from town. I don't have a car, or a phone, or a friend. When you're off working nights, it's just the cockroaches and me. The longer we live out here, the more we do the same thing every day. And the more distant I feel from you. What happened to the magic we experienced when we first arrived here?

Every day is cloudless, and after a while it's like the pale blue sky is mocking us with its unchanging smirk. Between the burnt-out flat and flowerless landscape, the unvarying sky, and *working at the same jobs every day, I feel like we're stuck on autopilot. The space between us is thick with stagnancy.*

As desolate as this desert of dust,

Kamala

If you keep doing the same thing over and over again, some part of you will go on autopilot. There is no intimacy when you're on autopilot. Instead of being fully present to what the moment is asking, you're just doing what you think is needed.

When we think we know all there is to know about a person, we stop trying to uncover who they are. Doing something completely out of the ordinary can prompt the process of discovery and bring us into fuller presence with the person in front of us. Whatever you tend to do the most, I encourage you to switch up your behaviors. That way, you are always fresh, always alive, and not getting stuck in stories or ideas about how the world is.

The world is constantly changing and pulsing and growing. Our stories swoop in to try to crystalize the world into being the way our minds think it should be. In reality, what was true a moment ago may not be true now. When we shift our perspective and do things out of character, we make space for newness to come in. We stop looking at the world for what we think we know of it and start seeing it for what it actually is moment by moment.

If you keep looking at your partner expecting them to behave in certain ways, you'll never get to be surprised by them and you'll never know who they truly are. If you look at your partner like a mystery waiting to be discovered and you get curious about who they are moment by moment, you create spaciousness for love to flood in.

Roadmap to Intimacy—Try Something New in the Bedroom

1. If your lover is not fully emotionally and mentally present with you, where are they? Their tension and attention is hiding somewhere in the body. Explore their body to find where their tense and tender "hiding spots" are. With loving presence, rub these areas to call your lover back to you.

2. Find the areas on your partner's body that feel unguarded and the most "alive." These areas are so alive with sensation you can literally feel it! Caress these spots and invite these areas to expand to your lover's entire body.

3. After you find the spots where your lover is "hiding" and "alive," put one hand where they are hiding and one hand where they feel alive. Connecting these two spots can be like flipping an electrical circuit to turn your lover on.

4. Less tension equals more flow of energy and better sex! Slow down; get out of your mind. Prepare a hot bath for you and your lover. Make your space beautiful. Let warm water melt away your tension and stress. Breathe slowly and deeply while you tell each part of your body to relax until your whole body is complete.

5. Sometimes the body can shut down or become too "melted" if it encounters too much heat from a bath. So prior to sex, another option is a warm shower with a minute long cold rinse. This can re-invigorate

the body and help to release stressful emotions.

6. Try turning your attention inward for five minutes and then turn our attention towards your mate to look at them with fresh eyes. Give your undivided attention to your lover. When you lovingly witness your lover with every aspect of you—your heart, your mind, your spirit, your everything—you create a caring space that wraps around you both to feel safe and protected. This allows you to explore each other and even transform your fears into love.

7. Set aside a time once a week to focus on connecting with your partner. "Date night" is a time to rebuild connections and open the possibility for making love. Having a set date night allows you time to prepare for physical intimacy, and can be as simple as bathing together or as elaborate as a fancy dinner.

Boundaries

Jediah,

Your co-worker's boyfriend, Ryan, invites me out rock climbing. We spend the day flirting and bloodying our knuckles on jagged rock. I feel weightless and free as I scale huge boulders, and I enjoy the attention as I look down to see him gawking up at my harnessed ass.

We watch the sun set over the desert on top of a boulder we just conquered. The colors bleed together like a painting made from dust. As the sun waves its final goodbye behind the washed out mountains, the breeze of a lightless landscape kicks up. On instinct, my body moves closer to him. I think of you and wonder if you're on your way to pick me up soon.

Ryan and I make our descent and strip off our harnesses. As we wait for you, he builds a fire and the night comes on strong. The moonlessness of the desert and the blaze of the fire make it seem as if he and I are floating in an orangish globe. We banter and I feel alive with a slender coolness that only a day of rock climbing can invoke. He moves close to me. The flickering shadows on his face shake me with a timidity that I try to hide by flirtatiously weaving my hair between my fingers. He grabs ahold of me and sinks his teeth into my neck. He bites confusion into me.

I hear a rumbling in the darkness that sounds like your muffler-less car.

He thrusts his hips against my clothed thigh a few times and lets out a squealing moan, "I'm about to cum!"

My body stiffens and the confusion intensifies. I wonder how I got here. Moments ago I was flirting, and now this oversized man is thrusting on me and jizzing in his jeans. He collapses limply down next to me, moments before you emerge from the night and step into the fire glow.

I freeze. I am certain you were watching us from the darkness. Ryan scrambles to look busy tending to the fire. My belly drops with unbearable guilt as your eyes penetrate me. In that moment time stands still. You're the first to break the silence.

"Did you guys hear those people having sex?"

I know you're referring to Ryan's sounds, and I am wondering if this is you fishing for a confession.

"No." My voice cracks as I squeak the sound out.

"I've been looking all over this campground for you."

Another wave of guilt washes over me.

I say a hurried goodbye to Ryan, and it isn't until the next morning that I tell you that Ryan and I were sexual. I spend the next few weeks before I leave Joshua Tree trying to repair *the damage I've done to you and to Ryan's girlfriend. Guilt repeatedly punches me in the stomach.*

Three weeks later, I find myself on Salt Spring Island in Canada. I'm sitting alone in a park writing and enjoying being in a place where I don't know anyone.

A hippie man walks up, "I've been watching you."

Without any other words he leans close to me and grabs ahold of my shoulders. His hands knead my body, sore from sleeping on uneven and unpadded ground for the last week.

I give in until my eyes roll back in ecstasy and I fully surrender to this stranger's hands. I am like a puppy on my back nestled in his arms when a shadow casts over me. I look up to see sunlight curling around a figure. Through the haze of my bliss and brilliance of the sunlight, it takes me more than a moment to realize it's Ryan standing over me. I stop, the hippie man stops, and Ryan just hovers there not saying anything.

A wave of guilt washes over me, as though the universe sent this man fourteen hundred miles to remind me of the pain I cause when I don't have clear boundaries. I think of you and the pain that bled through your eyes in the few weeks before I left Joshua Tree. Of Ryan's girlfriend and the betrayal she must have felt, of Ryan's burly body thrusting against me, and of my own body unwanting and rigid under his grip.

As the shock of seeing Ryan subsides, it's replaced by, "Of course."

Of course I would see Ryan fourteen hundred miles from where we fooled around, in another country, while in the arms of a stranger. I know now, without a shadow of a doubt, that the universe is ever-so-gently giving me a choice. Either be clear on what my boundaries are or keep hurting myself, and the men I give my body to.

The answer is pretty clear,

Kamala

You are in charge of how you do and do not want to be touched. When it comes to our bodies being touched, we should only allow what we feel a resounding "yes" to receive. If we try to bypass what we are authentically wanting moment by moment, we don't create space for others to step up and meet us.

Our boundaries are the container in which we find the freedom to open. Our boundaries are necessary in order for us to get what we really want. Our boundaries are the banks of a river and our desires are the river itself. In order for our desires to flow the way we want them to, we need boundaries. Without boundaries, there would be constant flood damage.

In order for us to trust others, we need to find their authentic "no." You can't fully trust someone's "yes" until they can say, "no." If you want to know whether or not to say, "yes," to something, wait until there is a resounding "yes" throughout your whole body. Your "yes" is essential for someone else to be able to trust you. No matter how intuitive someone is or how well we think people should know us, people are not mind readers. If we don't know what we want, we should slow down and breathe into ourselves. We ask the other person to slow down until we know we are ready to move forward.

Intimacy is rooted in deeply honoring ourselves and our own bodies moment by moment. If we are not honoring ourselves, if we are not present with ourselves, we can't have true connection with another. We might be afraid to ask people to slow down. We might fear others may get impatient with us, and they very well might. But having someone be impatient is far better than overriding ourselves and doing what we think the other person wants us to do. Intimacy is about being so present and connected with ourselves that we can't help but be fully present and connected with another.

Oftentimes people skip cultivating closeness with self or the other person and jump right into sex. When building intimacy, sex is the very last thing that should happen. Sex is letting someone all the way into our world. It's allowing them to weave into the fabric of us, and there they will stay. Once we have sex with someone, the energetic ties we have to that person don't go away. We are intertwined with them. We ingest them. There is a happy meeting place, between looseness and frigidity, where we can be both hold our own desire and the other person's desire.

Roadmap to Intimacy—Discovering Your Boundaries

1. Find a comfortable and safe space alone or with a partner.

2. Bring all your awareness within. Take deep breaths and notice what is happening inside you. Take a search light within as you breathe in and really explore what you're feeling and sensing.

3. Now breathe all your awareness to your environment or to the person in front of you. Notice as much as you possibly can. How much are you aware of yourself compared to how much you are focused externally?

4. Practice maintaining both internal and external awareness through breathing. As you strengthen your ability to be aware of yourself while simultaneously being aware of others, it will become easier to know what your own needs and boundaries are.

♥ Bonus: Practice saying, "no" more often. Say, "no" without explanation. If you're not completely excited about something, say "no". Practice your, "no" until saying it becomes easy.

Breaking Out of Old Stories

Dear Jediah,

Sitting around a fire, the reflections of light cast shadows on a circle of strangers. Oddly there is no music, no lone guitar, no slight drum beat. There is just the crackle of burning cedar as a dozen and a half people settle in and are hypnotized by the flames. My body aches. It's screaming for touch. I haven't seen or felt you for so long, I've almost forgotten what touch feels like. I look up from the wrench of my body and scan the circle. I know there is someone here who can help.

I see a quiet bearded man hiding behind glasses and sitting back from the circle. I have this knowing that he's the one who can help. Without introducing myself, I ask if he wants to do a massage exchange. He agrees.

Suddenly, he reaches one single finger out and touches my shoulder blade. An electric shock shoots through my whole body... somewhere between an orgasm and a rush of lightning. I spin around and look at him with delight and confusion.

"What did you just do to me!?!"

He smirks slightly, "What do you mean?"

He lays another finger on my lower back. Again, the voltage moves through my whole body as if waking up my cells. Each movement is more effective than if he were deeply massaging every muscle.

For the rest of the night, I convulse as I feel the gift of his touch being downloaded into my own body. I don't understand what is happening to me, but it feels like every cell in my body is being broken open and a new bit of information is imprinted in. I've never felt hands like his.

When you touch me, you only go for what gets you off, alternating between my ass, breasts, and cunt. It's like you don't even see the rest of me.

When I wake, I have a skill I never had before. My hands pulse as though they are made of vibration. I touch as many people as I can. I have no money to get back to the States, so I put up a sign in the park "Massage by donation". I instantly get customers and when I touch them, I feel as if we are merging. It's as if my hands can penetrate their skin, and unravel every twisted place within them. I feel their bodies as if they are my own. As they let out sighs of ecstasy, I let out sighs as though feeling everything that they feel.

I'm not the same person anymore. I know I've been trying to break free from you for years, but now I know, without a shadow of a doubt, I can't keep fogging up my brain, mind, and heart. I need to give up drugs, including you. I can't keep numbing out and blaming others.

I am coming to you to end things for good. My strength and sureness sends you into a tirade. You yell and punch your fists through every wall. I marinate in the clash of destroying you in order to choose a healing path.

I hitched out of your town with a shaky smile. Feeling lighter and heavier than ever before. I feel a weighted agelessness spread over my whole body.

The only thing I can do is keep moving forward,

Kamala

Stepping into who we want to be requires the courage to leave behind who we've been. Walking a path of growth and intimacy is not easy. We are faced repeatedly with a choice of either hanging out in our comfort zone or pushing our edges of growth. Moving closer to who we want to be requires us to grow beyond the stories we've created.

Stories are narratives we tell ourselves and others that are based on assumptions and past experiences. Stories are not truth. We all have stories that we believe. Stories about what it means to be loved, what it means to be beautiful, what it means to be a man or a woman. We create stories in order to feel a sense of safety, and help us be vigilant against being hurt. Stories separate us from the truth of who other people are and who we are.

We create stories to feel that we exist, to constellate an "identity" that replace our true nature. We lose awareness of this nature as the mind develops and the wounds of childhood accumulate. As we unwind our stories, we arrive more at our perfect selves, before we were ever hurt. An example of how a story is created—your mom leaves you when you're a kid, and you make up a story that you must not have been good enough to make her stay. Then, for the rest of your life, you battle the story that you're not good enough. You see the whole world through the clouded lens of not being good enough.

"I have too much belly fat, I must not be good enough. I just got dumped, I must not be good enough. I feel lazy, I must not be good enough."

Stories are lies that we believe to be true. They limit and contract our experiences. In reality, yes you have fat around your belly. So what? Yes, you got dumped. That was him doing what he needed for himself. Yes, you feel like lying down when you think you should be working, then lie down. It doesn't make you lazy. It makes you present to the authentic desires that are arriving in the moment.

So little of what we believe about ourselves is the whole truth. We all have experiences and traumas that shape the way we perceive others and ourselves. Whenever we experience a trauma, it has the potential to shape how we see the world.

Let's assume that 90% of what you think and feel about yourself and/or your partner is skewed by your past experiences. Imagine that you've been wearing thick glasses your whole life that make the world blurry. When you are present, authentically expressing and letting go of stories, you are essentially cleaning your glasses so you can see the person in front of you for who they really are in this moment.

So many times I've heard clients say, "I thought I knew him. How come I didn't see what a jerk he was right from the start?" I guide my clients to "clean their lenses" so they can clearly see who is in front of them.

A powerful practice to cleanse your lenses and break out of stories is to focus on gratitude. When we find what is good about our struggles, and find appreciation for them, we give ourselves the opportunity to step into the gift of the moment.

Gratitude gives birth to love and can take situations that seem challenging and fill them with insight. When you are in a state of gratitude, you open yourself to the richness that love has to offer, and stories can melt away. Expressing gratitude can feel vulnerable, but it offers opportunities to dip deeper into the well of love.

Roadmap to Intimacy—Appreciating Your Way Out of Stories

1. Journal about or share with your partner one harmful thing you believe about yourself. It could be: "I'm not good enough," "I'm not lovable," "People always hurt me."

2. Share with your journal or a partner how this belief has benefited you. How has it kept you safe? What gift has it brought into your life?

3. Appreciate yourself for having that belief so you can be where you are today. Notice how the belief shifts as you're grateful.

4. Pretend you don't have that belief anymore. Pay attention to how your body naturally wants to move and what sounds you naturally want to make when you're not operating from this story. Let yourself move your body as though you no longer have this belief.

5. Share how that experience was for you. What do you appreciate about the experience?

♥ Bonus: Gratitude is also essential for passion. How are you supposed to be in the mood if you or your mate isn't showing the appreciation that you feel both you deserve? Teach your partner how to love and appreciate you for the amazing being that you are. Every day, tell your partner at least three things that you are grateful for about them.

Summary & Quotes to Share

In order for us to bust out of old patterns, we need to be willing to ditch our stories, try something different, and approach the world with curiosity.

Busting Out of Old Patterns

❖ One of the best ways to break out of old patterns is to do something unexpected.

❖ When we approach our patterns from a state of relaxation, we break the walls of the rut we've dug for ourselves.

❖ If we take superb care of our bodies, hearts, minds, and emotions, we have way more access to the gifts we have to share.

Longing

❖ Longing can create an aching within that causes us to crave someone the same way we crave a drug.

❖ We can shift how much we long for someone, just by shifting our relationship with longing itself.

❖ We can have the same relationship with fulfillment as we do with longing.

Curiosity is Key

❖ If we stay open and curious about what each moment is bringing, we can dissolve our fear of being hurt by others.

❖ Curiosity about each moment creates intimacy.

❖ Sex is expansive when we treat it as though it is our first time uncovering what feels good, what makes us stir inside, and what beckons the other into love.

Beyond Words

❖ Bodies are constantly speaking through posture, minute muscle movement, facial expression, and breathing rate.

❖ Enhancing our internal awareness can help us translate what other bodies are speaking.

❖ People won't feel threatened if we're breathing deeply and approach them from a calm and relaxed space.

Try Something New

❖ Doing something out of our own ordinary can prompt a process of discovery and make us more present with others.

❖ Looking at your partner like a mystery waiting to be discovered, and getting curious about who they are each moment, creates space for love to flood in.

❖ When we shift our perspective and do things out of character, we stop looking at the world for what we think we know and start seeing it for what it actually is.

Boundaries

❖ Our boundaries are necessary for us to get what we really want.

❖ If you want to know whether or not to say, "yes," to something, wait until there is a resounding "yes" throughout your whole body.

❖ If we are not present and honoring ourselves, we can't have true connection with another.

Breaking Out of Old Stories

❖ As we let go of our stories, we arrive more at our perfect selves, before we were ever hurt.

❖ When we find what is good about our struggles, and find appreciation for them, we give ourselves the opportunity to step into the gift of the moment.

✉ Share on Facebook and Tweet @KamalaChambers

THREE

ELLIOT

Releasing Past Hurts

Meeting Elliot took all the newness that was waking up inside me and gave it a safe harbor to anchor in. We met each other with a child-like wonder which gave spaciousness for the past hurts and pains to surface that I had spent years trying to smoke and drink away.

On my twentieth birthday, I starting school for Energy Medicine and was eventually hired as a lead instructor at the institute. I was called to let go of past hurts and own my gifts. I saw how the willingness to wake up my inner gifts was essential for deepening intimacy.

The majority of our relationship was spent floating between the San Juan Islands. As soon as we gave up being nomads of the sea, and tried to settle down on a secluded off-the-grid island. The seas of change rose to split us apart.

Child-Like Wonder

Dear Elliot,

The first time I see you, I think to myself, "I am so screwed."
We see each other in the grocery store, of all places, the moment
we lock eyes, we don't look away from one another until we are
finished checking out. Our gaze says everything. As I walk away
from the store, a curiosity about you takes over, and I find myself
wondering about you often.

I don't see you again until we find ourselves around the
same crab feast fire. I know right away that you don't recognize
me in the distorted lighting, but still you invite me to spend the
night on your boat. We board a damp zodiac and whine our way
through the night. The warm breeze moves through us, and I sit
on the bow of the tiny skiff with my head thrown back as though
soaking up sun rays. The moon is fat and bright and illuminates
the water before us as though we are gliding over a silver path
of liquid mercury.

I don't know you, or where you're taking me. I study your
broad and muscular body. No one knows where I am. Breathing
in the salty air, I decide it's okay to trust you all the way. My
intrigue for you outweighs my fear of you.

We pull into a completely secluded harbor off an island with no houses. We board your twenty-six foot cruiser and shuffle around to sit across from each other at your kitchen/office table. We stare into one another.

I'm the first to break the silence, "Do you remember the first time we met?"

"Yes, we met around the fire."

"No, we met in the grocery store"

Your face lights up and your whole body opens, "That was you? That was you!"

You look at me like the prince who just discovered the Little Mermaid's voice to match the woman. You fall in love with me in that moment. We take each other in with child-like wonder.

You butter my insides with your deep brown gaze. It's a look I'll come to know too well. And after that look always follows a truth that I'll never be able to deny, even when I want to. You speak with such a steadiness that I have to shift in my seat to try to squirm out of the discomfort of truth.

Without even kissing, you and I play next to one another all night long. We melt into innocents, like children playing games. Our hands are curious and unending. As we rock to the rhythm of the changing tides, we discover places of youth-filled lightness waking inside of us.

The discovery unfolds,

Kamala

When we meet someone with child-like wonder, we have the opportunity to discover who he or she is in present time. When we are in our playful innocents with others, we drop our expectations and past experiences and arrive with who someone is right now.

On the path to cultivating intimacy and awareness, we can easily forget about playfulness. A quality of us that is often overlooked in relationships is our inner child. The inner child represents parts of us that may have gotten stuck at a certain age of emotional development due to a trauma, such as neglect or abuse.

The inner child holds aspects from childhood that were ignored, repressed, or suppressed. Aspects of us that never matured past puberty may dictate our behavior as adults. The child can be selfish, reactive, chaotic, immature, needy, dependent, and demanding. If the inner child continues to be ignored, these traits may rush to the surface and try to sabotage our relationships. On the other hand, if we integrate our inner child into our lives, we might experience more creativity, intimacy, and aliveness.

Our inner child also holds our childlike joy, freedom, spontaneity, and carefree ways. As we acknowledge the inner child, we can begin to walk hand in hand with them.

No matter how well our parents did their jobs, they could never completely fulfill our needs when we were children. Now though, we have the opportunity to re-parent ourselves—to give ourselves the love, affection, and attention we missed out on in childhood. We get to listen to ourselves so that we're heard, to hold our own inner little ones when they're sad, and to give them the opportunity to play.

Roadmap to Intimacy—Ways to Nurture Your Inner Little One

❤ What things does your inner child like to do? Make a list. Do something everyday that helps to nurture your inner little one. Our inner little ones may love the opportunity to play, make noise, be carefree, dance, sing, look for the magic in nature, or laugh at stupid jokes.

❤ Why is intimacy so scary sometimes? The first place you experienced intimacy was with your parent or primary caregiver. With them you were vulnerable, reliant on them, and where you were supposed to feel safe. Write a list of descriptive words about how you felt with your caregivers as a child.

For example, "With my caregivers, I felt: neglected, loved, frightened, cared for."

Examine everything on your list. How are you recreating these feelings in your relationships now?

❤ Aspects of you that never emotionally matured past certain traumas that occurred when you were younger may dictate your behavior as an adult. Try writing in a journal as an opportunity for the emotionally undeveloped parts of you to be expressed so that unhealthy cycles don't continue in your relationships.

❤ Sometimes our inner little ones just need an opportunity to express and be heard. To set up a dialogue between you and your inner child, write a question to her with your dominant hand, and write the response from your child with your non-dominant hand.

❤ When you're feeling hurt or sad, chances are you're inner little one needs some coddling. Don't try to rush past your feelings. Spent time with your feelings. Dialogue with yourself as though you are both child and loving parent. Touch your own body the way a nurturing parent would touch a hurting child. Allow your inner little one to be soothed by your love.

Releasing Past Hurts

Elliot,

You and I dance around each other for months before we decide to really do this thing together. I start school for Energy Medicine on my twentieth birthday, and I hitch there with a backpack full of books and no idea where I'll sleep for the first intensive week I'm there.

Going to school for Energy Medicine is like spelunking and unearthing all the shit I spent my whole life trying to bury. I'm told we can only help heal another when we have chosen to heal ourselves. I go on a deep dark dive into my issues.

I come to you with my brokenness, and fears and breakdowns, and with everything I am forced to face in the fires of self-healing. You hold me through it all and I somehow know, in your arms, I'm going to be okay.

Everything I spent my life blaming on other people comes crashing down. I can no longer deny that I am the creator of my own world, and I am the one who has made all this happen. You are like slow-moving honey that coats my pain and lulls me into an ease. I begin to rebuild myself, ever so slowly, and when I do, I build you into my foundation. You are a builder and I imagine you helping to lay the floorboards of who I am. There is no way to go around or dodge the pain anymore, all that is left to do is feel it and walk right through it.

There are no more drugs to turn to and no way
to escape my own pain,

Kamala

At what point do we stop having issues? When do we know we're finally "healed" enough to be in a good relationship? The path of healing never ends. We never get to a point where we stop having issues or triggers. Intimacy will continue to bring up reactions, upsets, pains, and the "ugliness" in others and us. And it's all beautiful. It's all part of the curious experience of being human. It is not about eradicating all the reactions we don't like. Intimacy is about fully integrating who we are. It's about our willingness to repair with our partners. It's about finding the right response at the right time.

Intimacy is not about getting over our issues, but rather about tracking our own nervous system and learning how to regulate it so we can have a relevant response moment by moment.

Getting upset with your partner for forgetting to pick up a lemon at the store is not a relevant response. Sure, anger is welcome, and it makes sense that you would be frustrated, but the reason you are feeling anger is not relevant to this situation. Perhaps you've felt let down many times in your life, and when you're let down it says to you that the other person doesn't care enough about you to remember your needs. Your anger is not relevant to the situation, but rather is making you aware of your want to feel loved and your need to feel important to your partner.

What is a relevant response then?

A relevant response would be if you trip in the middle of the street, and a car is coming and you're suddenly afraid you're going to be hit by that car. That fear is necessary for you to jump up and take action. If your nervous system didn't kick into a sympathetic response, you probably wouldn't jump up to get out of the road.

Intimacy and healing happens when you continue to move toward a relevant response. There is little time where we are actually in danger. Our work is in calming the nervous system down to a state where we are naturally tranquil. When your nervous system is calmed down, you don't perceive the world as dangerous. You don't interpret the things others say to you as an attack.

If we attempt to connect with another when our bodies are constricted, it is harder to connect with who they are. When we are highly tense, our own nervous systems are hijacked. Subconsciously, people will sense the tension in our bodies and they will become tense and often respond as though we are a threat. If we are relaxed, then biologically we don't appear to be a threat.

The more we are present to each moment, the more our bodies calm down. We can start to track what dangers are actually occurring moment by moment. We step out of past dangers and sink into what is truly happening right here and now. When strong emotions arise, we can give them space to be here. They're not bad. They merely indicate a deeper need that is longing to be heard. When feelings come up, we have an opportunity to inquire within and ask ourselves if this feeling is completely relevant to this situation. 99% of the time it's not.

We can feel our honest emotions and ask, "What is it that I am really needing right now?"

Then we have the chance to pause, breathe, wait for the answer, and give our precious selves the attention we need.

Roadmap to Intimacy—Healing Scars

We all have scars both seen and unseen, moments in time where trauma left a mark on our physical or emotional bodies. Both physical and emotional scars distort your energy flow. Turning our attention toward something helps energy flow into it. When we give attention and care to our hurts, we can nurse that injured part of ourselves back to wholeness.

1. In a safe, warm and comfortable space, take off your clothes and lay down.

2. Place a generous amount of oil on your hands. (Coconut or sesame oil is best.)

3. As you oil your hands, allow them to be illuminated with tender, loving energy.

4. Allow your hands to gently and tenderly massage oil into every scar on your body as if you were tending to a baby. (The oil helps to conduct energy. Oiling your scars on a regular basis helps energy to flow through that area of your body more freely.)

5. Breathe into the loving touch you are receiving. These hands are not trying to take anything from you, and have no agenda. There is no need to think about the ways you've been hurt, this time is to allow your body the opportunity to receive whatever it may need right now.

6. Slowly breathe into your hands, allow them to gently and tenderly massage the oil into your pelvis. When your pelvic floor is open, it is easy to connect with the earth. You have access to more energy and the earth's energy can come alive in your body. Blossoms from flowers rooted in a garden last longer than flowers in a vase.

Seeing Our Fears and Moving Forward Anyway

Dear Elliot,

We've been floating for months. Suspended in a twenty-six foot cabin cruiser love bubble. We go to shore to dig clams, gather oysters, and pick berries. The rest of the time we anchor in secluded phosphorescence-drenched harbors. Once a month, I hitch to the mainland to spend an intensive week at the healing school. I come back to you blasted open and with a deeper understanding of the mysteries of the universe.

As autumn bleeds into winter, the air wafting off salty inlets crisps. The long promise of cold causes us to nestle even deeper into a cocoon together. My studies call me into the dark crevices of my subconscious. With you everything is slow-moving and calm, but on the inside I feel a darkness bubbling.

For the new year we cross Spieden Channel to the tiny off-the-grid haven of Stuart Island. As soon as we touch shore, a storm rolls in. Snow falls and the jaws of millions of violent waves chomp greedily. You're not willing to risk our lives to get back to San Juan Island. Through the snow, we hike to a cabin an acquaintance owns. We find a way to break in without doing damage. I assess the food rations in their pantry while you build a fire to cut the brittleness of the air.

We spend days by the glow of the fire, watching the snowfall and the waves thrash against the shores. Across the knives of the sea, we can see San Juan Island, as if taunting us...so close, yet seemingly impossible to get to. When the pantry runs low, I claw my way through the snow in the garden and unearth beets and chard. I go to the beach and knock oysters lose from rocks until my fingers are numb and bloody.

There is not much else for us to do but stay warm and for me to do my homework, which painfully prompts me to dredge up childhood traumas. With each page of homework, I am whittled to deeper levels of memories until I drop right into the center of the lies I've believed about myself.

You sit in the peach glow of the firelight, watching the snowfall. The cabin is saturated with a calmness that matches the goose down comforter tossed over the landscape. I wonder if all the things I'm not saying are thickening the air between us? Currents of pain well in me, more violent than the waters you're afraid to cross.

In the candleless corner I quietly sob over memories. I've been trying to hide these parts of me away, but out here there is no escaping myself. I've been so terrified of you leaving and rejecting me that I haven't even given you a chance to know me.

My face becomes a beach at low tide. The salt of my tears slowly dry.

I look out onto the perfect landscape. The swirling of storm clouds, the turrets of snowflakes, the ever-changing vast and grey sea, the thick and fleshy Madrona trees bending their branches under the weight of snow. You're nestled under blankets, scribbling building designs in your notebook. This moment is too beautiful to not lean into. As I soak this in, the pains of the past start to dissolve.

Love is bigger than pain,

Kamala

Intimacy is being willing to leave behind what we think we know for what we can discover. When we lean into our life experiences, we move closer to what each moment offers. When we are willing to say goodbye to who we think we are, we open ourselves to embrace who we truly are.

We've all had wounds. We've all had hardships. And ALL of those hardships hold a gift, if only we choose to embrace them. We will continue to repeat unhealthy patterns to try to validate our limiting beliefs.

Our minds are like a computer. Easily programmed. By age eight, our minds are 85% programmed. Think about that. By the time you're eight years old, you have already established most of the belief systems that will dictate your behavior for the rest of your life. That means, if you didn't have pleasant experiences as a child, you most likely created negative beliefs about yourself that are affecting your health and happiness to this day.

When we are wounded as children, some part of us accepts that the pain we felt was normal. We then subconsciously seek that experience again. We will continue to try to find ways to validate our limiting belief until we bring it into consciousness and work to change it. The good news is that when you develop new belief systems you can reprogram your mind. If you're not conscious of your thoughts, your subconscious mind can fuel everything you do. When we practice being aware of our thoughts, then our thoughts won't be off running wild. We can reprogram our minds by interrupting our negative thoughts that have been stuck on repeat.

As we repeat thoughts, our brain synapses will keep firing on the same pathways. The more we repeat thoughts, the more these brain synapses fire together. If we change our thought processes, we can actually rewire our brains. Our neural pathways start to fire in new directions, and it becomes easier to think things in a different way.

When we notice thoughts that don't make us feel good, we can choose to replace them with thoughts that feel better. What you are attracting to your life can be an indicator of your thoughts and belief systems. If you are a successful person, you have the belief systems to back that up. If you are attracting unhealthy relationships, it is because you believe that is what you deserve due to your past experiences. Right now you can reprogram yourself with positive affirmation and replace old thought patterns by affirming the new path you are choosing.

The mind is tricky and it's not easy to stop thinking the way we are used to. The more we interrupt our thought patterns, the more we give ourselves a real chance at intimacy.

Roadmap to Intimacy—5 Ways to No Longer Let Negative Thoughts Run Your Life

1. When you feel good in your body about something, say, "Fuck yes," to it when you want to say, "Yes".

2. When something doesn't feel good to you, do not justify saying, "No." Just say it.

3. When your mind is over thinking, pause and pay attention to the sights, sounds, sensations, and flavors the moment is offering. Pay attention to what you're feeling in your body.

4. Keep asking yourself, "What else is there to discover right now? What do I need in this moment?"

5. When you find your mind cultivating stressful stories, interrupt what you're thinking. Put your foot down. You don't have to see these thoughts through. Just stop yourself, whatever you're doing, and do and think something else.

Owning Our Gifts

Dear Elliot,

The founder of the school has taken me on as a mentee. She is training me to take over her position so I'll be able to teach in-depth on Energy Medicine. I head off island for my final week of training and to celebrate graduation. Instead of being in the classroom, though, I've been in the hospital. My grandfather had a stroke and is in a coma. I wish you were here with me to hold me through this.

Before I entered his hospital room, my aunt pulled me aside, "I know you're graduating this week. This is your graduation now. Please help my dad."

I step into the room and turn on my energetic vision. I scan grandpa's still body. All of his energy centers are shut down and barely functioning. I look up towards his head, and he's standing outside of his body. I can see the energetic outline of him, as clear as I see his body lying here. I know that he's not coming back. No matter how hard I try to pull him back into his body, I know he's on his way out.

For a few days I sit in a hospital conference room with my dozen aunts and uncles as they discuss what to do. I try to tell them he's not going to wake up, but my words are muffled by the clamor of fatherless emotion. At night, when the sterile corridors have quieted, I go to my grandfather's side. He patiently waits for his wife and children to let him go. I take out a notepad and paper, and scribe a question on the page?

"Grandpa, is there anything you want me to tell anyone?"

And then I wait until I feel the pen lift itself in my fingers and words start to fill the page. The pen moves for thirty minutes before I can even get out the next question.

"Grandpa, what have you loved most about your life?"

Again, I wait for the pen to move and quiet my mind and body enough to hear him. The pen moves itself. I ask more questions until I'm too exhausted to go on. My aunt and uncle enter the room drunk and transmuting their tears to laughter. I hide the crinkled and filled pages.

This is crazy Elliot! I wish you were here. Your steady wisdom is like an oracle card. You always know the perfect thing to say. I'm scared to read what grandpa wrote through me, and I have no idea if I should share the words with my already distressed family. As my uncle banters with a nurse, I pull out the pages, and peek at what was written. It takes me a few minutes to realize that half of the page is written in Spanish. My grandpa knows Spanish, but I don't. Sure I spent two months in Costa Rica, but all I learned was how to order food and ask where the bathroom was. I swear grandpa did this so I couldn't second-guess myself.

I know my aunt speaks Spanish. Alcohol and emotion have her crumpled on the floor. I find a sentence that seems easy enough to pronounce.

I stammer, "What does, 'el otro lado es bueno' mean?"

She looks up at me and smiles as though she knows why I'm asking, "The other side is good."

Grandpa and I share her smile. I look into him standing there and he says it's time for him to go. He waits until morning to fully crossover; once all twelve of his children are here. With the last breath he takes, it is so palpable that his soul leaves his body that even my most conservative uncle recognizes it.

A few hours later I meet you at my school with tear stained cheeks. I cry as I fall into your arms. I was called to trust my abilities more than ever before, and this trust seeps into my connection with you. You and I stand amongst the clamor of excitement of my fellow graduates peering into each other. We take a deep breath together and somehow my ability to open to you widens. I feel as if I am being held by my own gifts, and I can no longer hide them. Today I graduate. I graduate as a practitioner and as a teacher. I graduate from playing small. I graduate from hiding out.

I'm here now,

Kamala

In order to deeply connect with another, we are called to fully own, love, and embrace the most spectacular aspects of who we are. If we want to be met by people who are inspiring, we must be inspiring ourselves. Intimacy can seem like it is just about connecting with another person, but really intimacy is about fully connecting with all of who we are.

Intimacy calls us to fully own our greatness. If we want more from another, we need to be willing to own more of our awesomeness. When we identify what our greatest joys are, we set ourselves up to have relationships that we're excited about every single day—and passion for life makes us magnetic! We have the most success when we're passionately engaged in activities and relationships that makes us feel happy, fulfilled, joyful, and in love with life.

Many of us have bought into in the popular mindset that in order to be successful and happy, we have to put our heads down and work extremely hard at something that isn't guaranteed to bring us joy. Being connected to your joy is the greatest gift you can give yourself—and it's the greatest gift you can give to your relationships. When you're living your joy and you're steeped in a life that brings you happiness and fulfillment, you'll draw in uplifting relationships like a magnet. Your magnetism and enthusiasm will make people want what you've got!

We can wait for others to rise up to meet us or we can rise up and meet ourselves. If we want another to rise up and meet us, we must completely embody what we desire in ourselves. If we want to be met by an authentic masculine presence, it requires us to fully be in our authentic feminine presence and vice versa. The more we step up, the more others will step up. If we want someone else to really show up for us, we have to fully step into ourselves.

Roadmap to Intimacy—Owning Our Gifts

Either journal or share with another:

1. What makes you feel the most joy in life? You'll know you're onto something good when your mind is clear, your body is relaxed, and you feel the most delight.

2. What is most sexy, fun, and juicy about you? Brag about yourself!

3. What are the five things you love most about yourself?

4. What makes you feel sexy? What can you do to feel sexier? Every morning do something to promote your sexiness. It takes just as much energy to put on a stained t-shirt as it does to put on a flattering top.

Poison of Blame

Elliot,

We make love for the last time. Neither of us knows it's our last, yet your hands touch me like a stranger. You move around my body like it's the first you've ever explored. Your hands are timid mysteries. The room is too dark to see you and I wonder who's touching me. You explore as though you will find something in my body that you've been looking for.

What is it?

What are you looking for?

What do you want?

My words are laced with confusion and urgency.

More than anything, I want you to speak. I want to cure the silence that had inflicted your tongue these past few months. You say nothing. You stay a silent stranger. With large rough hands, the dimness of your silhouette seeks something that I know you won't find. The light of dawn only reaffirms what I suspected was brewing in the darkness. Your vacant and unblinking eyes are as distant and cold as your wordlessness.

You slough off to build someone else's house for the day, and I'm left with a feverish urgency. I spend all day pounding the earth, digging up crabgrass, and trying to make rocky ground into fertile soil. I bought a massive amount of veggie starts from a sale at the one room schoolhouse, with plans to make a garden in front of our new home. I moved to this tiny off-the-grid island with no electricity to live a Walden Pond dream with you.

Today is my attempt to plant myself. Perhaps if I dig deep enough, I can root myself here. Perhaps you'll come home and see me planted. See my blossom and want to nourish, water, and watch me grow. In pink and white flowery underwear, a thin matching tank top, and furry winter boots, I claw at the earth. Like an animal I claw with bare hands at the dusty ground.

When you left this morning there was only a field of grass and my sheer anger and pain. When you come home, there are several veggie starts rooted, an herb garden unburied, and me covered in dust and exhausted by a nonstop day of desperately trying to root myself here. As you approach I must seem like some wild beast. Sweaty and dirt-stained, half-naked, wild-haired, blackened-fingered.

We sit near the new garden, my hands are fists full of earth. The fields of clovers around us are on fire with crimson blossoms. You confirm it's really over between us. Until that point, my tears had been dammed behind long formed walls. The dam breaks. Sobs spill from some undiscovered place within. You wrap yourself around me. If you could, you would have used your heart to mop up the tears. You carry me to the outdoor wood-fire bathtub and lay me under a tree while you build a fire in the hollow beneath the tub, and fill it with water from the hose. I huddle fatally, streaming a river of sorrow and loss.

When the water is warm enough, you peel the few clothes from my dirty body and lay me in the tub. Your muscular arms lift me effortlessly. The water makes me howl and the gentleness of your touch makes me sob even harder. Although the water is warm, I shiver violently. The bottom of the tub burns me as the fire rages beneath it. Smoke and steam mingle as it rises through sunlight streaming between trees. From the womb of water, tears cast a strange luminescence on the pristine world around me. It is like being in a dream and I pray that it is. My cries echo through blackberry brambles, sting the thickets of nettles, and reverberate through the forests. You quietly sit, back against a tree, looking calmly toward the sky.

In the morning, I take a small powerboat off the island. Before I board, we stand there awkwardly in the silence. What do you say to someone you're closing a chapter on?

Like always, you know what to say, "I don't know when we'll meet next, but I know we will be better than now."

I have no more tears left. I climb aboard the small ship and stand peering off the back of the boat. The engine churns the waters, and as I speed toward my new life of unknown, I watch my old life disappear. You and I both stand staring at one another until we become tiny dots. You, strongly rooted in your new homeland, and me, once again, flying over unsure waters into another life I'll have to make up.

I watch my heart crush as the coal of your eyes fade in the distance. My dreams crumble as the pristine cliffs of Waldron Island slip away. As I turn the bend and see the last glimmer of you, I wonder if you're celebrating or if your heart's churning questions, "Did I do the right thing?"

I want to hate you right now, but I can't. I trusted that you would be here and continue to love me. I want to blame you for my pain right now, but I know it was here long before you were.

Goodbye love,

Kamala

If we want true intimacy, we have to be willing to own all of ourselves. This means stepping out of blame and moving into self-responsibility; taking full responsibility for everything we are thinking and feeling moment by moment.

The only person you are really required to trust is yourself. If you trust yourself it really doesn't matter what other people do. If you keep showing up and loving them, then the way others are treating you or not treating you doesn't matter. We think it's important to trust others, but the only trust we can have for others is that we trust they will be themselves. Maybe we have an idea of how someone should be and when they don't live up to our stories, we pull away and say, "I can't trust you." When someone's actions don't line up with our idea of them, then our idea of who they are needs to shift. It's not that they are untrustworthy; it's our stories about them that have perhaps been untrue.

When we feel hurt by others and lose trust, often times we want to blame them. We want to say our pain is someone else's fault. In relationships, blame is poison. Blame will eat away at relationships, claw out love, and replace it with resentment.

When we trust ourselves, we don't have to worry if others are trustworthy, and we can step out of blame. We don't have to worry if others are living up to our stories about them and blame them for not being what we think they should be.

Roadmap to Intimacy—Breaking Out of Blame

Typically, the more intimacy you have with someone, the more old, unhealthy patterns rise to the surface. As your bonds and connections deepen, so must your commitment to hold your partner in love and non-judgment.

Notice, share, or journal about what your predominant thoughts are about your mate each day.

What are you blaming them for?

Be curious about why they do what they do and how you might play a part in creating what you're unsatisfied with.

Share as often as possible what you appreciate about them.

Summary & Quotes to Share

Often times our past hurts can distort how we see our partners and ourselves. By stepping into a sense of child-like wonder and owning our gifts, we can clear away past hurts that have been clouding our view.

Child-Like Wonder

- When we are in our playful innocence with another, we drop our expectations and past experiences and arrive with who they are right now.
- Until we give ourselves the love, affection, and attention we missed in childhood, aspects of us that never matured past puberty can dictate our behavior and sabotage our relationships.
- We can give ourselves the love, affection, and attention we missed in childhood.

Releasing Past Hurts

- Intimacy is not about getting over our issues, but rather about tracking our own nervous system and learning how to regulate it so we can have a relevant response moment by moment.
- When we're tense, people sense it and unconsciously respond as though we are a threat.
- When feelings come up, we have an opportunity to inquire within and ask ourselves if this feeling is completely relevant to this situation.

Seeing Our Fears and Moving Forward Anyway

❧ Intimacy is being willing to leave behind what we think we know for what we can discover.

❧ We can reprogram our minds by interrupting our negative thoughts that have been stuck on repeat.

❧ The more we interrupt our thought patterns, the more we give ourselves a real chance at intimacy.

Owning Our Gifts

❧ Intimacy can seem like it is just about connecting with another person, but really intimacy is about fully connecting with all of who we are.

❧ When we identify our greatest joys, we set ourselves up to have relationships that excite us every single day.

❧ Passion for life makes us magnetic!

Poison of Blame

❧ If you trust yourself, it really doesn't matter what other people do.

❧ When someone's actions don't line up with our idea of them, then our idea of who they are needs to shift.

❧ When we trust ourselves, we don't have to worry if others are trustworthy.

✉ Share on Facebook and Tweet @KamalaChambers

FOUR

FOREST

Sacrificing Yourself to Be With Someone Else

While Elliot and were together, Forest and I were best friends. When Elliot ended our relationship, Forest didn't waste anytime and swept in to confess his love. I felt blown over by the intensity of his passion and it quickly seemed like I was sacrificing important aspects of myself to be with him.

We were both surprised at how drastically being intimate changed the dynamics between us. The fundamental differences between us started to surface. I was a lead instructor at an institute for Energy Medicine. His skepticism of my work and addictions seemed to directly oppose my path. We struggled with how to connect with each other.

When we found a common passion through Lakota traditions, it was clear that connecting physically, emotionally, mentally, and spiritually were all essential. In order to gain clarity on my life, I went on an intensive vision quest. During that time, I felt Spirit was guiding me to surrender to Forest's love. I finally felt like I could relax into the relationship. The more I embraced our partnership, the more I was able to see what was missing. Shockingly, it seemed that what I needed was something that directly opposed the guidance I received from Spirit.

Sacrificing Yourself to Be with Someone Else

Dear Forest,

You come rushing towards me with the fury of a winter storm. It's only been two weeks since your friend Elliot broke my heart, and you aren't wasting time. I feel disoriented by the way you move in and whisper two years of suppressed feelings heatedly into my ear.

I've always found you incredibly attractive, but it's all just too much too soon. I had no idea you were just waiting for your turn with me. When you jump to kiss me, my body starts convulsing. I am shaken to the core with your passion after two years of flirting foreplay.

I feel disoriented by your desire. It seems a moment ago I was riding a long a perfect wave with Elliot, and now, I'm being repeatedly hit by waves of your desire. I'm trying to follow bubbles to find the surface of myself, but as soon as I come up for air, you hit me again. I'm not ready for you.

I'm not ready for us, but I'm buckling under the weight of your persistence,

Kamala

Falling in love is like being swept away by a tide. After the disorienting wash of brain chemicals and gushing feelings of new love, there is a point in relationships where we may wake up and say, "Who am I? Where am I? How did I get here?"

We can lose sight of ourselves. We come out of the new love fog, and then start resenting the person in front of us for carrying us away in the first place.

So how do we navigate the tricky waters of love?

How do we know how much to give to others versus how much to give to ourselves?

Being in love with another seems like it's all about being swept away with the person. But really, being in love calls us to deeply listen, connect, and feel ourselves. Sure, relationships often ask us to make compromises, but this doesn't mean making compromises that pull us off the center of who we are. We can only give as much as we can be present to ourselves.

One of the main struggles I see my clients going through is feeling like they lose themselves in the process of being with someone else. I see many clients holding back in their relationship or even afraid to get into new relationships because they don't want to lose themselves.

We can avoid losing ourselves by knowing our greatest desires in life and continuing to make choices that feed those desires. Maybe your greatest desire is to give all you can to your child, feel deeply connected to yourself, or be in a loving harmonious relationship. Whatever your desire is, keep asking yourself for all your love choices, "Does this feed my desire or take away from it?"

Roadmap to Intimacy—How to Know You're Not Sacrificing Yourself

This can be done alone or sharing with a partner:

1. Think of a decision you want to make—one that has two potential paths.

2. Think of what it would be like to walk down the first path. As you think of this, notice how your body feels. Notice what happens in your mind. Do you get distracted, start thinking about other things, or is your mind clear? On a scale of 1-10, how joyful do you feel?

3. Now think of the other path. Notice what happens in your body, mind, feelings, and joy level. On a scale of 1-10, how joyful do you feel?

4. Flip back and forth between the two choices a few times. You'll know what path to chose by finding the one where your mind is the most clear, your body is the most relaxed, and you feel the most joyful.

Connection

Dear Forest,

Although you've been my best friend for two years, now that we've made love, everything seems to have changed. We're on a road trip driving across America and I feel like we're in a constant state of sibling rivalry. It's confusing that we've been so close for so long, and now that we're intimate, we're constantly pushing each other's buttons.

There are some fundamental differences between us that I can't seem to shake. By the time we're on Lake Michigan's shores, we're barely talking. You meet up with old friends and get caught up in a blaze of weed smoke. When you're stoned, I can't access you. It's like another person walks into your body, and you're not here anymore. Sometimes after you smoke, it takes you days to come back.

When I smoked, I often felt thick clouds crowd around me, and sometimes I would literally feel like I was being taken over. After you've smoked, your pupils change, your eyes dim, and I know it's not just you I'm dealing with anymore. It feels like such a conflict to be with you. I'm an instructor of Energy Medicine, and teach about how drugs tear the etheric web and leave us vulnerable for other entities to walk in and take over. Yet here I am with you, a man who actively puts himself in a position of being possessed on a regular basis.

I need to get away, and find my way to the lakeshore. It's like a tropical freshwater ocean with pine trees instead of palm trees. The sun is setting and dazzles the still waters with millions of gemstones. Sitting in the smooth sand, I wonder what to do.

From my questioning mind, I look up to see the most beautiful woman ever seen walking the waterline. Her hair the same color as the sand, and her curves match the subtle waves. My heart skips a beat!

She stops at my feet and looks down at me with eyes as lonely and blue as mine. We instantly connect and she invites me out dancing in Kalamazoo. I jump on the opportunity to spend more time with this Russian beauty. Before we go, she takes me to meet her husband, to convince him it's a good idea for him to let her go out. I get the impression she's a mail order bride, and she shares about how disconnected she feels from her husband.

We're out most of the night, salsa dancing with strangers. We press our bodies together on the dance floor and draw a crowd of hungry men around us. She slurps down drinks through a twisty straw, until she's too numb to notice the many hands groping her. Our dance turns into her slumped onto me while I slap away grabby hands. One man grabs her and pulls her close.

When they kiss passionately, I realize it's not their first time meeting. Sweaty and worn out at the end of the night, I wait in the car while they practically have sex on the hood.

I think about her husband back home—how disconnected they seemed from one another. And how diffused this beauty seems in the haze of booze. I think about you, having an affair with weed, and how impossible it has been for us to connect. As the car gently rocks from the bodies getting hot and heavy on the hood, I wonder what it takes for people to truly connect with each other.

What would it take for you and I to really meet; to break out of the cycle of fighting and start connecting?

I miss our friendship,

Kamala

We all want to feel connected. We all want to feel like we're a part of something more than what we think we know. But how do we do that? How do we filter out all the overwhelming inputs from the world long enough to really drop into a feeling of unity? How do we bridge the seemingly endless gap between ourselves and everyone else?

Connection extends far beyond a sense of familiarity, safety, and reciprocity. We can connect through our bodies, words, emotions, and energy. When we heighten our awareness of the subtle energetic world that we are all a part of, we open ourselves to experience deepening levels of resonance with others.

Everything is energy. Even Einstein said so. All energy is vibration. For all of us who have played a string instrument, we have seen that all vibration moves towards a state of entrainment, when two different vibrations find one common resonance. Everything in the universe is seeking to connect, entrain, and find that common meeting place where it can communicate.

All of our thoughts, words, feelings, and bodies are energy. That means that everything has its own personal vibration, its own song. Each tree, each blade of grass, each person has a song.

Think of yourself like an orchestra. Every organ, every cell, every thought has its own unique frequency and is its own instrument. All of the "instruments" of you play together to create your overall song. Within your own personal song, the frequency that is playing the strongest usually takes the lead. Our thoughts and feelings have incredibly strong frequencies, and often play the conductor in our personal symphony.

The song we are singing to the world depends upon what type of songs we draw towards ourselves. If we are putting out thought frequencies like, "I love my partner! They treat me so well," then we will draw in vibrations that match those thoughts. If we are emanating a frequency of gratitude towards another, they may entrain with our vibrations of gratitude. In turn, the collective song of gratitude will play louder within you and the other person.

We entrain with stronger vibrations. The stronger we are in ourselves, the more others entrain with our good vibes. Whatever vibrations you are emulating affects what you and others entrain to. You might have noticed this when someone walks into a room in a great mood. You might have had a hard day, but suddenly, just being around this person makes you feel better. That is a basic form of entrainment.

Our energy is changing all the time depending on our thoughts, feelings, foods we eat, substances we take, etc. The choices we make can dramatically shift our energy. The more we connect with ourselves and take care of our bodies, minds, and hearts, the more we raise our energy and can have more fulfilling relationships.

We are multi-dimensional beings, providing opportunities to connect on multiple levels. There is a tightly woven net of energy around humans. Theosophical author C.W. Leadbeater called this energy the etheric web. This energetic web acts as a filtration system between the dimensions. It filters out information from high dimensions, to protect our consciousness from opening to realms it is not ready to perceive. The etheric web protects us, and when healthy, can open gently, allowing us to experience profound levels of connection.

Without this etheric protection, people could be "overtaken" by energies outside themselves. Any harm done to the etheric web can create harm to the individual. Some things that may damage the etheric web are extreme shock, trauma, or fear. Damage to the web may be accidental or can be caused by repetitive habits. Substances like marijuana can manipulate the etheric web, and lower our overall vibration. Many drugs can have dramatic affects on our vibration, and using alcohol, tobacco, and even caffeine can damage the etheric web.

The etheric web is like a one-way filtration system. However, when the jagged energies of substances, such as drugs and alcohol are ingested, the physical and energy bodies immediately try to dispel these chemicals. The energy of the drug is then forced back out through the chakras (our energy centers where we process information).

Hallucinogenic drugs (and even marijuana) can tear open the chakras and burn holes in the etheric web.

Repeated drug abuse eventually destroys the chakras and etheric web. Therefore, energy from other realms can flood in without a filter. The filter helps us to comprehend information coming in. When information is received in a drug-induced state, it is often untranslatable to physical reality.

When drugs, such as alcohol and marijuana, are abused over significant amounts of time, a second reaction can happen to the web—a deadening of the senses. The damaged etheric web may become hardened. It ceases to be web-like and becomes more of a hard mass that very little energy can pass through. This deadening can make us feel painfully disconnected from others and ourselves. We can become numb, depressed, or hopeless.

Drugs can be a way to open consciousness in an unconscious way. But when they wear off, so do the insights, and you're left with the numbing effects of the after party. I used to spin in tangled realities induced by marijuana and hallucinogenic drugs. I had some great visions too; moments when the puzzle pieces of the universe seem to fit together. And in the next beat, the insights would evade me. Too soon the high would fade and I would forget the feelings and answers I had gleaned from the blaze of a drug-induced state.

After a long stint of bleak colored hangovers and highs and lows, both becoming progressively lower, I decided to try something different. Prying my consciousness open with the crowbar of drugs just wasn't enriching my evolution. I decided to give up drugs and learn about human energy systems. Attending the school for Energy Medicine showed me how to help raise people's own energy, simply with breath, movement, and intention.

I've found that the longer I go without drugs, the more naturally high I become. It's a kind of high without a hangover. With intention, breath, sound, and movement, I can now access, at will, the states I tried to enter with consciousness altering drugs,

Movement and breath can help loosen up and relax your body. Energy can't flow through a constricted body. When your body is soft and flexible, energy can flow through you more easily. Physical movement helps in opening, strengthening, softening, and grounding the body. When you get your body moving, you get your breath going, and thus you raise your vibration.

Freeform dance can be one of the best ways to get energy moving through the body. It is all about connecting with yourself and moving the way your body wants to move. It lets your mind move out of the way, allowing free expression and release of any holding patterns, mental and emotional heaviness that may be trapped in your cells.

Breath alone is the single most important way to move energy through your body. For anyone who has ever danced until you forgot your name, you may understand that breath and movement is the quickest way to achieve this energy movement. Oxygen feeds your whole body, and the energy of the oxygen is food for your energy bodies.

Roadmap to Intimacy—Seven Ways to Raise Your Vibe

1. Move your body! Put on some music and dance shamelessly. Explore how much you can express who you are with your breath, sounds, and movement.

2. Eat superfoods! Foods that are nutritionally dense can pack your body with nourishment and flood your body with life-force energy.

3. Hang out with people who inspire you and make you feel good. The more you spend time around people who lift you up, the more your energy will shift and start to match theirs. Pay attention to who you spend your life with. Typically, we energetically mirror the five people we spend the most time with. Hang out with people who you want to emulate.

4. Replace old habits and draining people. If you do something often or spend time with someone that brings you down, let it go. Your life and energy is precious. Take time to connect with new people, do exciting new things, and express your creativity.

5. Spend time in nature. Being in nature can help you feel alive again. Take time to take in the natural world. Let your senses come alive as you watch trees move in the wind, smell the perfume of flowers, or taste the bite of freshly picked rosemary.

6. Connect with yourself. When you're connected to yourself, it will be easier to feel what does and doesn't raise your vibes. Take space to be with your-

self. It doesn't need to be a dramatic retreat; it can be as simple as taking a deep breath.

Be with your own body and feel the delight of having someone give you unconditional love and attention. Let yourself know, "I'm here for you. I've got you. I'm not going to let you go."

Ask yourself, "What will make me feel the most amazing right now?" Be still and wait for the answer.

7. Have great sex! If you make love when you are relaxed and connected to your partner, it can be an amazing way to raise your energy even higher. When you make love, being physically tense can decrease your pleasure. Let your sex be free from just being a "tension dumping ground."

If you release your tension first, with regular vigorous physical activity, you will likely have far better sex far more often. Swimming, a workout, yoga, running, dancing or martial arts can all be good outlets for expelling tension in your body.

Sharing Passions

Dear Forest,

Now that we're at a Lakota Sun Dance Ceremony, our relationship makes sense. It feels like we finally have a common ground. We're with five hundred people all holding space for dancers who ceremoniously pierce their chests and rope themselves to a cottonwood tree. Here energy is palpable. Dozens of men spend days beating on drums so large they make the ground shake while hundreds sing Lakota songs in shrill and melodic tones.

Even you, Mr. Skeptic, can see spirits crowding around and feel the thickness of the energetic potency. Peter is dancing this year, spending four days out in the sun, with no food or water, sharp bone piercing this chest as he is roped to the tree in the center of a large arbor. Singing for him bonds me to him and opens me more to you.

With a common ground of prayer, doorways of connection start to open between you and me. For the first time, we find a sexual rhythm that wasn't there before. I've felt so disconnected from you for so long, it's been challenging to know how to intimately meet. With this common language merging us, we're able to connect with something bigger than just you and I. As we come together spiritually, our passion grows. The physical attraction as been here, but we just haven't been lining up on other levels. I'm seeing how necessary it has been for us to find a common passion.

Sharing our passions, we're sharing more of who we are,

Kamala

Passion cannot be spanked into creation. Passion is born out of connection. The deeper the connections, the deeper the passion. Unfortunately, most people are not taught how to truly connect with others or even connect with one's self. If we want to truly connect with another, we must learn how to listen to the subtle (sometimes not so subtle) aspects of ourselves first.

Taking moments to breathe and listen to ourselves is essential for passion. There are many different levels we can listen and connect on—sexual, spiritual, mental, emotional, and physical. Connection with self is essential for passion, and we need others to help us connect to ourselves even more. Others can show us how to love ourselves and touch ourselves in ways we've never imagined. All people are like mirrors to peer deeper into who we are.

Taking moments to connect in with our own feelings, bodies, and hearts gives us a chance to be fully expressed. When we express all of who we are, we give ourselves the opportunity to come alive in our passion.

Sexual connection can take less effort than other types of connection. Yet, if we nurture the other types of connections first, the relationship will have a more solid foundation than the tipsy ground of sexual turn-on. This is true even for long-term partners. Sexual interactions will be more passionate and fulfilling if you and your partner enter the encounter connected on all other levels first.

There are jellies and creams, laces and leathers, probers

and prodders galore to spice up your love life. With five types of female orgasm and 169 love positions to choose from, you'd think you could keep your passion alive. When focusing purely on the candy of sex, though, we can overlook the organic nourishment that lovemaking can provide.

Making love can be an opportunity for you and your partner to create beautiful synergy. It can be a doorway into uncovering important aspects of yourself; where you stand naked and undefended in the presence of love and acceptance.

Passion isn't isolated. When it wakes up in one area, it weaves through all aspects of our lives—sex, relationships, business, and creativity.

What is passion to you?

What does it mean to have passion in your relationships?

What do you think about igniting more passion through deepening connection?

Roadmap to Intimacy—Connecting on All Levels

Whether you've been with your partner for two days or twenty years, I highly recommend making an effort to connect on all other levels before entering sexual unity.

1. Physical Connection:

   Do non-sexual physically engaging activities with your partner like dancing, cuddling, or partner yoga. In these activities you have an opportunity to physically connect without the pressure of sexuality. This helps to build a sense of safety together, which is essential for connected loving.

2. Emotional Connection:

   Express your heart-felt desires to your partner. Allow the opportunity for you and your partner to share feelings. Compliment your partner on subtle details you notice about them. If they have pretty eyes, chances are, they've heard that complement a hundred times. Let them know that you notice the little things about them (like their earlobes). Focus on things that make them special to you.

3. Mental Connection:

> Engage in conversation about topics in which you both share a common interest and passion. Mentally collaborate on ideas, solutions, and actions you can take to enrich the topic at hand.

4. Spiritual Connection:

> If you have a spiritual practice, include your partner. If you don't, find ways to interact on deeper levels. For example, try chanting, meditating, or sharing prayers or gratitude's together.

♥ This may seem like an awful lot of foreplay. I promise you, though; the results will be a lot more fulfilling than wham! Bam! Thank you, ma'am!

Giving Men What They Need

Dear Forest,

I don't have a pen or paper so I am writing this to you with the clouds right now. I've been sequestered in the woods for two days and two nights. I'm tied to a cedar tree by a strand of 405 of my prayers, each wrapped up with tobacco in red cloth. I came out here to find a vision for my life. This is my hemblecha. My slender support person brought me up here with nothing but a wool blanket and a chanupa pipe and enclosed me in this five-foot prayer cage. The tribe of a dozen Lakota practitioners and you are holding space for me in the camp below. I've had no water, no food, no sleep, and I'm here to cry for a vision for my life.

The air is thick with mosquitoes that I am not supposed to kill in this space. The past few days, I've tried to breathe through the agony of being eaten alive. Even in the heat of the day, they violently swarm. I try to bury my claustrophobic head under the thick wool blanket in the ninety-degree weather. Sweating profusely, I beg to understand how this experience is supposed to be helping to guide me. Each time I peek my head out to gasp for air, I feel the sting of more bites on my face.

Too weak to swat them away, the mosquitoes feast on my face and body. I finally surrender into the agony when I have no more fight in me. I pray that eventually they all get full and leave me alone. I'm supposed to be here having some kind of spiritual revelation, but instead, I'm imagining these little bloodsuckers exploding from gluttony. Tasting the thickness of my thirsty tongue, I laugh at the irony. At least something is getting to drink.

You're heavy on my thoughts. Our relationship has been like a pestering mosquito that I've been trying to fight off since we started. We've been combating since the beginning, and I ask spirit what to do. The answers come to me in pictures drawn in the sky. Through the thick forest, there is a tiny patch of blue sky and swiftly moving clouds. The smoky shapes tell me a story of exactly what I need to do with my life.

The clouds shift and the next patch rolls in. I see the shape of a pregnant woman and I'm sure it's me. In the next set of billows, I see the profile of a man reaching toward the belly. The cloud hand and the cloud belly merge and create a bigger cloud. I'm certain now that you and I are meant to be together. Really together. Merging our spirits.

With the mosquitoes feasting, the clarity of the clouds, and my exhaustion from no food, water, or sleep, I surrender. It's time to stop fighting you. In this moment, it's painfully clear that I haven't been receiving you. Rather than embracing you for who you are, I've been holding onto hope that you will change. I fell in love with you for your potential, and every time I see you not living up to that potential, I fight you. I'm tired of fighting. I'm ready to see who you really are and find our lightness and fun again.

At dawn on the third day, my supporter comes and leads me into a sweat lodge to be cleansed by my own sweat. You and I are meant to spend our lives together. All that is required is that I stop resisting. My vision quest helps me to see that this is the life I've been asking for. All I needed to do was say, "Yes."

Finally fully saying, "yes," to you,

Kamala

It's hard to know who we're loving when we're set on loving someone for who we want them to be. When we focus on the greatness that is alive in people, we get to be surprised by the things in them that we'd otherwise overlook. So often a woman is blessed and cursed with the ability to see a man's gifts. She is cursed because it is easy to fall in love with a man's potential.

It can be painful to see a man's gifts clearly and know he's not living up to them. To call out a man's gifts, the woman must create space for the man to step. She can't nag her way into getting a man to come forward. Yet, the woman holds the key to help him step fully into his potential.

When we can access what people need, it is easier to maintain a connection to ourselves as well as others. To find out what people need often requires attentiveness, curiousness, and inquiry. On the surface level, someone may think they need cake, but their deeper need may be to feel more loved.

One of my mentors, David Cates, has led men's groups, helped thousands of couples and been in the field of Tantra and sexual healing for over forty years. Through his work, I learned about the deeper needs that both men and women have, and how when we meet those needs, we can show up more fully for ourselves as well as for the person in front of us. The following sections are adapted from his work.

How do we meet the deeper needs that other people have? Men and women are different creatures. Let's first look at what men, in general, need from women.

To open, a man needs to:
1. Know the rules of the game
2. Get rewarded with touch
3. Be invited to fully connect
4. Be able to play in mutual curiosity
5. Have his gifts summoned

Men Need to know the Rules of the Game

In order for men to feel safe, they need the game of the relationship to have clear boundaries and rules. This means the more straightforward and honest his partner is, the more he can relax. Men need to know what rules they are playing by. This requires a woman to communicate that she is here and physically present to the rules.

If a man is trying to figure out what a woman wants, he may have trouble being present, because he's busy testing boundaries. And if a man is testing boundaries all the time, then it's hard for the woman to open because she's busy trying to fend off his advances.

When she expresses what her boundaries are, he knows what he can and can't do. The woman might say, "I'm interested in making out with you, but I don't want to have sex with you tonight. Is that something you're interested in?"

That way, the man can decide whether or not he wants to play this particular game with her.

She sets up the rules of the game. This isn't about manipulating him or trying to control him. He can decide if he wants to play or not. If she has hidden rules or agendas outside of what she is communicating, it creates distance between them and neither of them feel like they can trust each other.

Oftentimes, beginning by stating a clear intention can create instant intimacy. It doesn't matter what the game is or what the intention is, what men want is a clear container. The clearer she is, the faster she can get to connection.

He will meet her when she can commit to being completely in the moment. When a woman steps all the way into herself, she becomes irresistible.

Men Need to be Rewarded with Touch

Most men want to know that their sexuality will be included. If she doesn't include his body, he won't feel safe. When a woman lays out the rules of the game and the man plays by the rules, then his reward is touch. If she just has sex with him or gets him off right away, he will feel like she doesn't respect herself, and if she doesn't respect herself, it seems likely she's not going to respect him. If she skips to the reward, he won't be able to fully trust her.

Creating the container of boundaries first, allows both the man and the woman to relax into one another. If she just hops to giving him the reward of touch, neither of them will get what they really want. She won't have the closeness she desires, and he won't have access to all of her.

If a woman isn't open to fully receive a man and he has an orgasm, he'll feel depleted. We all know the story about a man who cums, then rolls over like a beached whale—it's as if he wants nothing to do with her. He checks out mentally and emotionally. He'll need his cave time and withdraw.

When a woman knows herself, loves herself, and is so open and capable of receiving, she is able to embrace the man for all that he is. When she creates spaciousness before a man even enters her by letting him in energetically, into her heart, by the time she allows him into the sacredness of her body, he will be able to deeply relax into who he is as a man and as a gifted spirit.

Men and women both want to know they will be fully received. A man will often try to pound a woman's body to get her to receive him. A woman will often try to pound with her emotions to see if he can receive her. Both routes are tense and can be damaging. When they relax and allow their bodies to rest with another, they don't have to pound desperately to try and get others to receive them.

The female makes the rules and gives the rewards depending on how well he is doing. Women are required to be highly in tune with their own desires minute by minute and communicate them. When women communicate, they're not leaving room for interpretation. If the rule is you can flirt but not touch, and he starts to get pawsy, then the game is over. If she doesn't feel safe then he doesn't get the reward. A man needs to be able to respect that the woman is capable of creating clear rules in order to feel safe. A man feels safe when the woman sets the boundaries. Both men and women create the container together. Touch is his reward when he shows he is trustworthy. The trust is built depending on how well he can follow and listen to her physical and emotional rules.

A woman first needs to be clear on what her own boundaries are. This requires her to be deeply in touch with what she wants and be willing to stand by it. If she states a boundary and then doesn't hold it, she's sending a message that he can push her boundaries. When a woman is clear, a man can relax and feel safe with her. He knows what the game is, and can get a reward for playing well. A man can relax deeper with a woman when he knows she's not going to get scared away by his desire. And women can relax within themselves when they recognize that they can steer the desire in the direction they want. If women have loose boundaries, don't know what they want, or are not communicating, a man can't fully relax. Women need to be the banks of the river for men's desire to flow through. That means holding strong boundaries, and communicating what she does and doesn't want from the man.

Most women want to know first and foremost if a man is trustworthy. If he is trustworthy, then she can move into physical intimacy. If a woman bypasses the process of discovering his trustworthiness and just has sex with him right away, her body can't fully relax. And for women, relaxation is key to pleasure.

Women who jump into sex without intimacy do not give men what they truly want. Men want a place where every part of them is welcome. If a woman can fully receive him, there is no need for him to ever go outside the relationship.

In relationships we push against one another to see if the other will break. We test each other's strengths and weaknesses to make sure the other can receive us. In order for women to have man come closer, they need to give them space to move closer. If she is leaning in all the time, tensely trying to be fulfilled, there is no room for him to come closer.

A Woman's Roadmap to Intimacy—
How to Get a Man to Open

1. Sit with a man without touching him.

2. Check in with yourself and become clear on what you do and don't want in this interaction. You can make it as simple or playful as you want.

3. Open your eyes and look at the man in a way that communicates that you are clear on what you want and you are clear about your boundaries. Express what you want and what your boundaries are with body language or words. Be clear on where you want the two of you to end up in the next five minutes.

4. Invite the man to take a journey with you to get to where you want to go.

5. If he stays within your boundaries, reward him with touch.

Men Want to be Invited to Fully Connect

When a woman merges the clarity of her intention, her heart, and the reward, she has access to her full power with every man she meets. Women draw men in when they give up their doubts, fears of heartbreak, stories, and feelings of being a victim. The more a woman gives up her stories, the easier and more fulfilling it is to meet the right man. The more she is emptied of her inner struggles, the more she is met by him. The more she arrives with him in the moment, the more success she'll have with him. If she gives up 5% of her stories, she'll have 5% more success.

As she is willing to leave behind her stories, she can relax more with the man for who he is. Rather than her reaching out and wondering what he is thinking and feeling, she can simply be clear about her own desires and intentions. Women often want to pry men open so they can emotionally access them. He doesn't have the opportunity to share what is going on for himself when she is desperate for him to share. He needs space to step into sharing rather than being pulled into sharing.

Men need a solid container, and they need to feel their freedom. They need to know where the boundary edges are. The container helps them to feel freedom so they can fully relax into the rules of the game.

Men want to provide for women. When women are clear with men about what they are wanting, men can relax and give women what they need. A woman must be open to receive what the man gives. She creates the container and he fills it. If she appreciates him for filling the container. Even if it's not in the exact way she wants, he'll keep filling it, providing, and feeling his value.

Men Want to Play in Mutual Curiosity

Play and fun are essential pieces for a man to fully open. When she opens up and invites him to explore what is going on for her, she invites him to open his curiosity. When she is present, she invites him to be present. Once the connection is flowing between them, they can play and have fun.

It's not necessary to endlessly process or talk about feeling and issues in order to connect. Endlessly processing will actually push him away. Connection can be fun rather than heavy and weighted. Bringing him all the way into the moment requires that a woman sets aside her old stories and be present for him in the moment.

When she opens to the free-flow and enjoyment of the moment, she invites him to be fully present in his body. Women who get what they want are all the way in their bodies. They say with their very presence, "I'm here. This is what I'm going to create. I deserve it." The more she can be clear, the quicker they can get to the play. Men need to have play. They need to know that they can be little boys. They need to know that all of them is going to be included.

Being playful means being willing to switch things up. If she's not getting the results she wants, then she has to change her approach. She has to be willing to keep trying something new until she can get him to come out and play. She can explore how goofy or silly he can be or how much she can make him laugh.

If he's accustomed to going fast, then she needs to invite him to slow down. If he's used to heavy emotions, she needs to help him find playful lightness. If he's used to talking about everything, then she can invite him to communicate without words. Switching things up keeps the perspective alive and fresh. It keeps the relationship opening and not forming ruts.

Men Want their Gifts Summoned

A woman can summon a man's gifts once she feels deeply connected to herself. She becomes the model and he'll follow along. The clearer she is about what she does and does not want and what the reward is, the faster they can connect. When a woman is sure of what she wants, she can be trustworthy, and his heart and soul will pour into the moment.

He will become fully present when she becomes fully present. If she wants him to ravage her, she needs to surrender to him. When a woman steps all the way into herself, her clarity, and her desire, she becomes irresistible. If she is wavering, he'll waiver. Women are the ones who steer. They are the rudders of the boat. With their words, movements, intentions, actions, and feelings they direct men. Many women want men to take charge, but the only way for a man to fully take charge is if she is directing. She needs to point him in the right direction so he knows where to go, what to do, and how to do it. This does not mean that women need to control men. This means that women need to work with men and simply point them in the direction.

A great example of how women can steer men is seen in many forms of partner dancing. Men are the leaders. Men are the ones who tell women exactly how to move. A good follow won't back lead or move until the leader directs her where to go. A good follow will only move when the lead either directs her or creates space for her to add in her own play.

In partner dancing it seems like the men are calling all the shots, but really, the best leads are the ones who are listening to their followers and leading them only where they want to go. A good lead needs to be able to listen to her body so he knows what she is capable of. A good lead will be in tune with her breath and her hips and what she is opening to. A good follow will be so present with her body that she is able to communicate what she wants without words. This level of non-verbal dialogue takes practice and presence to learn. You don't have to be a dancer to learn it. The same principles can be applied in all male/female dynamics as well as in the bedroom.

A Woman's Roadmap to Intimacy—Summon Him Partner Exercise

1. Go within yourself and find the deepest parts of you as a woman.

2. Take deep breaths, making a sound as you exhale as a way to invite him to breathe with you. Breathe into your womb, heart, yoni, and root. Can you open yourself to fully receive him? Take a deep breath and feel your own heart and body opening. Can you move into yourself as goddess, move into yourself as queen, royalty, divinity, mother earth? Find the deepest parts of your own inner feminine. Be clear about your boundaries.

3. Begin to summon him forth by embodying the compliment of what you want to draw out of him. Be the goddess to his god. The woman to his man. Be aware of the power inside you as a woman.

   Create vastly eternal openness that has space for all of him. It doesn't matter if he knows his own depth because you can create space in yourself to draw out the depths of him he didn't even know he had.

4. Move your body in a way that brings more of your own essence online. If it's not moving, men don't notice. If you're sitting quietly and waiting for him to pay attention, chances are he won't. Until there is some motion, even verbal, men most likely won't notice.

Move in a way that conveys how much you want to receive him. Men want to be received, discovered, supported, and encouraged in developing the unique gifts and genius that they have.

It's hard for a man to tap into his gifts without you creating the space. His gifts have nothing to do with how "successful" he is in the world. His gifts are about who he is underneath all his stories and masks.

Let him feel the deep love of the feminine. Just be for a moment—be the fertile ground where he can land, and show him that all of him is welcome and wanted.

5. Invite your man to relax into this experience and be summoned. Trust that something deeper than his personality can rise up from within and be more present in the world—all of his successes and confusions and clarity. Invite him to fully arrive and respond to the power of your invitation.

6. Questions you can both ask yourselves are, "How much can I open? How much space can I make? How much love can I bring?"

7. Breathe deeply together. Inside this connection make space for your own humanness, your own personality, your own limitations. Let yourselves sit together with all of it for three more breaths, breathing together and making a slight sound on the exhale.

8. Let yourself notice the sensations in your body and your feelings. Let yourself feel the potency that is present.

9. To go deeper, create playfulness and exploration. Remember that what makes this container sacred is your agreement that you are all the way present for this exercise. This connection has a beginning, middle, and end. Release your partner and reclaim your own power.

10. Thank him with appreciation and enjoyment—honoring what you shared.

11. Share what you learned about yourself in this experience, and invite him to do the same.

Giving Women What They Need

Dear Forest,

I've been feeling a relaxed calmness since my vision quest. I haven't been questioning if we should or shouldn't be together. Things are good between us. I'm not fighting us anymore. I've been spending a lot of time with Peter. With him I get to say all the things I can't say to you. He has this way of honestly sharing what is going on for him that makes me trust him in a way I haven't been able to trust you. He's able to really hear me, and I feel like whatever is happening within is okay. What I'm about to share is painful to write.

Today, while Peter was listening to me, I realized...I'm in love with him. And in that moment I knew I couldn't be with you anymore. It is painfully clear that I'm not being held in the ways I want to be. I will not leave you to be with Peter. I don't believe in leaving one person to be with another. Peter is just showing me what I've been longing for, and I know I'll never find it with you. He shares my dreams and passions, and I'm able to open more to him than I ever have with you.

Even through the clarity of the moment, I feel confused. I'm angry with Spirit.

Why did I do that vision quest?

Why did I spend two days starving in the woods, getting eaten alive by mosquitoes just to have Spirit tell me that my life with you was perfect?

It seemed so clear I was on the right track!

The answer I'm getting is as clear as the visions that told me to be with you, "In order to change, you have to accept what is."

These past two years, I've been resisting this relationship. It's been an inner battle to be with you. And now that I have finally relaxed into what is, it's time to let us go. I need to be with someone who can hold me with a tenderness and a spaciousness that you can't

I love you. You'll always be my friend.

It's time for me to go,

Kamala

Women can seem like such complicated creatures that have ever-changing instructions on how to care for them. Once men discover the special sauce to give women exactly what they need, they'll realize women are far less complicated than they seem.

When a woman is tended to, she can be a wellspring of generosity and love. When women are fighting to get what they want, the currents of emotions can push them around inside. Women are like the ocean. Their emotions are deep and stir unexpressed feelings to the surface. A man trying to control, stop, or solve a woman's emotions is like man trying to control the ocean itself. The ocean can be calm and the ocean can be violent. If a man can be a stable lighthouse, the storm will pass, and as soon as the waters settle, they will be clearer than before.

Being a lighthouse for a woman's ocean of emotions and discovering her deeper needs are just a few of the tools that can help build a solid haven where women can rest and fully come alive in their brilliancy. Just like men need women to fully activate their gifts, women need men to tap into their profound potentials to love.

To open a woman, she needs to:

1. Make Space
2. Be brought into her body
3. Have the man lead with vulnerability
4. Be affirmed and go slow

Making Space

Creating space for a woman is about creating emptiness. In order for a man to create emptiness for a woman, he needs to empty himself. Men want to provide for women. They want to feel like they are able to solve problems and find solutions. But when a man tries to solve a woman's problems, and jump in with advice, it's often received as though he is telling her she is too stupid to try and figure it out on her own.

Men's natural impulse is to look for what they can do to solve the problem when really they need to look for how they can listen. Unless she's asking for something different, a man listening to her, and letting her arrive at the answers on her own, is the best way he can help solve her problems.

To help a woman create space, invite her to talk. Ask her questions until she starts to open up and share. If a man can just listen to her for ten minutes, without interrupting, without trying to change anything, her brain chemistry will start to shift. She'll be able to clear out some of the mental gunk that is clogging up her view.

Some women need this clearing time every day. If a man can't provide it for her, he can encourage her to connect with other women with whom she can have this time for verbal clearing. It can be rather terrifying for men to listen as the storm of a woman's words and emotions are raging. But if he can track her body, it can help him stay calm through the process. He'll be able to see a noticeable difference in her body if he lets her speak uninterrupted. The man can actually see her breathing deepen, her muscles relax, and the lines in her face soften.

The advanced version of listening to a woman is empathically repeating back what he heard her say. When he shares what he heard, he can ask her if he got it right, and keep asking her to share until she feels truly understood.

Women have a deep internal wisdom that often gets clogged with emotional backlog. The best way for a woman to solve a problem is to empty out her emotional backlog so she can access her own intuitive wisdom. Most often, women don't need a logical solution; they just need the space to hear their own wisdom. Women are intuitive creatures, and when they have the space to listen to that intuition, they can access a wisdom far more customized to what they need.

For men to hold space for women, they need to realize the best way to solve the problem is to listen and let her clear out enough so she can access her own wisdom. No matter how brilliant a man, his insights are tiny compared to the wisdom she can access when she is held and has cleared out enough mental gunk to hear herself.

A Man's Roadmap for Intimacy— Creating Spaciousness Within a Woman

1. Sit down with your woman and let her know that you are present with her through your eye contact, gentle touches, words and attentiveness.

2. Ask her to share with you what is going on for her. Encourage her to speak. Keep your body relaxed so she feels safe.

3. Once she starts speaking, just listen. Don't interrupt. Don't try to make her feel better. Don't give advice. Just listen to her. She may need 10 minutes or more of you just listening.

4. If you find yourself starting to get overwhelmed, pay less attention to the words she's speaking and more attention to how her body is shifting as she talks.

5. Once she is finished, ask if there is more that she would like to share.

6. Repeat back the main feelings that you heard her say. Ask if you got it right. Ask if there is more. Keep asking if there is more until she feels understood.

Bring Her Into Her Body

A man needs to know he is getting results, and the results are written all over her body. Her body is constantly communicating about how open she is to him.

Her body will speak to him through:

The wetness of her yoni.
The deepness of her breathing.
The loosening of her muscles.
The smiling of her face.
The steadiness of her eye contact.

If she is deeply listened to, her ability to experience pleasure expands drastically. When women start to go into emotional turrets, men often short-circuit. Their minds are often single-focused and women's minds are multi-tracked. The problem is that men try to track everything a woman is saying. But she is speaking a different language... one that most men can't understand. It's a deeply emotional multi-layered language that often is rooted in insecurities that have nothing to do with the present moment. These insecurities are often linked to past experiences that she may unconsciously assume he knows all about.

A man can try empathically repeating what he hears from his woman as a way for her to know she is understood, but if she needs to go on a long vent, or if he starts to get overloaded, he can shift his focus to her body rather than her words. He is invited to just notice her breath, facial expression, tension, and relaxation. Her body will tell him exactly how to listen to her, whether it is staying quiet or whether it is reflectively listening and empathically repeating back what he has heard.

The more the man tries to solve her problems, interrupts her process, or takes what she is saying personally, the longer he draws out the process. If he can give her at least ten minutes of solid, deep listening, there is a good chance that is all she needs. Otherwise, that same issue can drag out for hours and sometimes even years until he provides her with that space she needs. If he keeps being curious and invites her to share, it lets her know that he wants the muck inside of her so he can turn it into fertile soil.

If she isn't relaxing, he needs to relax his own body more. Men are often physically stronger. When he is tense, her body might instinctively perceive a threat. If he is relaxed, than she can relax because her body won't feel like it's in threat of being attacked.

She will scan his body to make sure that she is safe. She will try and track what is happening within him to know if it is safe for her to open. When he relaxes his body, she relaxes. All this happens on such minute and biological levels that it's easy to consciously miss.

A Man's Roadmap to Intimacy—
Helping Her Relax into Pleasure

1. The amount of pleasure she can experience is equivalent to how deeply she can relax. When she can let go of jumbled thoughts, relax tense muscles, disperse the heavy emotions, she has room for true pleasure to shine through. Support her in helping her to feel safe, let go, open, and sink into the pleasure of the experience. Moving slowly and confidently will help her to know that she can relax because you're listening to what her body needs.

2. If you both practice relaxation techniques throughout the day, like deep breathing and yoga, you'll be more centered and available when it comes time to be with each other. Increasing your relaxation can also make it possible for you to have passionate sex for longer periods of time.

3. Find ways to help her body to relax. Offer her neck or foot rubs, draw her a bath, or caress her gently.

4. In order for women to feel sexy, they need outlets to release emotional stress. If she hasn't had physical activity invite her on a walk or bike ride. As the emotions release, she'll feel lighter, more confident, and sexier.

5. In order to deeply relax into the bliss of the present moment, she must feel safe. When she feels safe, she can relax. When you are relaxed and present with her she'll know that you're paying attention..

Lead with Vulnerability

When men verbally share all the things they don't want a woman to know, they allow themselves to be vulnerable. When he is honest and real, she'll trust him more. When he can share what is vulnerable and scary, he invites her in. Women want to hear what is happening for men. When men can be vulnerable, honest and open about what they are holding back, it's like a pressure valve releases in the woman.

Men can lead with vulnerability by speaking about what is happening in their bodies in real time. If a man is trying to hold space for a woman, this is not a time for him to monologue. It's a time to get vulnerable and share what is happening right here and now and let her know he is not holding onto it.

Men may want to create connection physically with their bodies, but if they're not expressing what is going on for them, women pick up on that. They'll know he is not being transparent and they won't feel safe. If she doesn't feel safe, the woman's body won't fully open to the man's. She might let him physically inside her, but he won't be able to emotionally penetrate her.

Whatever a man is not sharing, the woman feels. If he wants a detective constantly trying to dig information out of him, all he needs to do is hold in his secrets. If he wants her open and relaxed, he needs to be willing to share all the things he doesn't want to say. One of the biggest mistakes men make with women is thinking they can keep secrets or hide parts of themselves. Being with a woman is being with a magnifying glass. She will often know something is happening for him before he even does. She will respond to his internal world no matter how well he thinks he is hiding it. If he's not sharing, it will drive them both crazy. It will drive him crazy because she will keep digging, and it will drive her crazy because she'll feel there is something he's not sharing. And she won't trust him.

When a man is not expressing himself, it puts all the weight of expression on the woman. When he opens, it allows her to relax and know that she doesn't have to be the one to carry all the emotions. Sharing about the past doesn't bring you closer to someone until you're able to share what is happening in the present. When they share about the past, they can start by stating, "What this situation reminds me of is…" This kind of sharing can evoke empathy.

Leading with honesty is essential for both men and women. What is it that we are actually wanting from the other person? Do we just want to sleep with them? Do we just want to sit and talk with them, or hug them, or have no interest in having sex with them? Both men and women need to be clear about what they are wanting and be courageous enough to share. When we share it's not from a place of expecting others to fulfill our desires, but from a place of inviting the other into our world.

A Man's Roadmap to Intimacy—Share Your Vulnerability

1. Share with your partner, "What I am most afraid to share is…"

2. As you share, take deep breaths and notice what is happening in your body.

3. Share with your partner, "What I notice in my body when I share this is…"

4. Take three deep breaths together and feel your body relax.

5. Share with your partner what positive shifts you feel now that you've shared.

Affirm and Appreciate Her

For a woman to fully open, she needs to feel the man's deep appreciation for her. Women are beautiful, desired, and sought after creatures. Most women have been objectified, violated, molested, or even raped. So often, men find their favorite parts of a woman and zero in on those parts—her tits, her ass, and her cunt. When getting sexual, women can be in a constant state of vigilance or emotional checkout trying to manage how their body might be violated.

Most men have never had any intention of violating a woman in any way shape or form, but the history of violation is stored in her body. And if she ever checked out during sex, or didn't speak up when she wasn't enjoying something, she's experienced sexual violation.

Women want to feel adored. They want to feel special. If a man is just focused on her tits and ass, how is that supposed to help her feel special? When he narrows his focus on these areas it doesn't invite her to feel that he is really here with her, for her, and not just the parts of her that he can get something out of.

The man must be willing to look at her as a whole. The eight thousand nerve endings in her clitoris extend far beyond that pea size mound hidden in the folds of her mystery. Women have incredible orgasmic potential. Women have the potential for every part of their body to feel as much pleasure and sensation as the clitoris. Many women will never unwind and relax deeply enough to experience this kind of pleasure, but this is where the man comes in.

If he can lose his agenda when touching her, relax his own body, and touch her entire body as if it is as sensitive as a clitoris, he can open her to relax into pleasure. For many men, speeding things up and almost violent levels of stimulation are what they think will create more pleasure. But both men and women have the potential to draw the focus from their genitals and feel that aliveness and pleasure in their entire body.

Sometimes we get flooded, distracted, or overwhelmed. When that happens it's time to take a pause. Slow everything way down in order for her to access her entire capacity for pleasure. The more relaxed a woman's body is, the more pleasure she can experience.

A Man's Roadmap to Intimacy—Ways to Show Appreciation for Her

- ♥ Compliment her on something that is completely unique to her. If she has pretty eyes, don't just compliment her eyes, find something unique about her that maybe no one else has, like her ear lobes.

- ♥ Let her know the things she has done that you value. Share your gratitude for her.

- ♥ Slow down with her body and let your hands explore all the crevices, valleys, mountains and vast landscape of her skin. Let your hands go slowly with her and really be attentive to all of her body.

- ♥ Take pauses to make eye contact with her, kiss her sweetly, and brush the hair from her face. Find ways to touch her softly even when you're not trying to be sexual with her.

Summary & Quotes to Share

When we are in love it can be easy to get swept away by our feelings. In order for us to not sacrifice ourselves in relationships, we need to be connected to not only what we need, but what the other person needs as well.

Sacrificing Yourself to Be with Someone Else

- ✤ Being in love calls us to deeply listen, connect, and feel ourselves.
- ✤ We can avoid losing ourselves by knowing our greatest desires in life and continuing to make choices that feed those desires.

Connection

- ✤ When we heighten our awareness of the subtle energetic world that we are all a part of, we open ourselves to experience deepening levels of resonance with others.
- ✤ The deeper we connect with ourselves and take care of our bodies, minds, and hearts, the higher we raise our energy and can have more fulfilling relationships.
- ✤ When you get your body moving, you get your breath going, and thus you raise your vibration.

Sharing Passions

❖ Connection with self is essential for passion with others.

❖ There are many different levels we can listen and connect on—sexual, spiritual, mental, emotional, and physical.

Giving Men What They Need

❖ For deep intimacy, men need to know the rules of the game, be rewarded with touch, be invited to connect, play in curiosity, and have their gifts summoned.

Giving Women What They Need

❖ For deep intimacy, women need to make emotional space, be brought into their bodies, have the man lead with vulnerability, be affirmed, and go slow.

✉ Share on Facebook and Tweet @KamalaChambers

FIVE

DOYAL

Sharing Anything and Everything

When I got together with Doyal, I knew he was all wrong for me, but I just couldn't seem to help myself. As we dove deeper into the relationship, the distance between us only seemed to widen. I wanted to speak up and share all the things that I was holding back, but I was too afraid.

I thought if I didn't express myself or let him get too close, he couldn't hurt me. That couldn't have been farther from the truth. The more I hid away my feelings, the farther I felt from myself. It wasn't until Doyal and I were pushed to the edge of a traumatic situation, that all the unexpressed feelings between us erupted like a volcano.

When I was able to turn love on within and express my aliveness, I started to draw immense amounts of love into my life.

Through the lessons in this chapter we'll explore how and why it's essential to let others into our inner worlds, to be completely honest with ourselves, and to fully express who we are. When we stop suppressing what we're feeling, we give ourselves the freedom to talk about anything and everything. When we are fully expressed, the most awesome aspects of ourselves can shine through and we become magnets for love.

Inviting Others In

Dear Doyal,

I am pretty surprised by you. Whenever I see you, you're singing. At parties your guitar and songbooks draw crowds together. I belt out with my out-of-tune voice with all the passion and exuberance that I can. You kind of seem like a nerd, and it isn't until I see you with your shirt off that I start to think differently. Normally you are buried behind glasses and a beard and a heavy coat and brown old man shoes that you wear with white tennis socks.

You invite me over to your cabin that we take an aspen forest trail to get to. You come in from the outdoor shower. Your chest is muscular and bare and still pebbled with water droplets. You take my breath away. Between your body, the way I feel when we sing together, and the calming nature of your cuddles, I fall in love with you quickly.

All these feelings welling within are unexpected. You're not at all what I think I want. You smoke, you drink, you hermit yourself away in the forest. You even use Crest Toothpaste! But something happens when I'm in your arms. My body melts. And when I look into your eyes, I feel as though I am looking right into God's eyes. Between your arms and eyes, I am done for. I am yours. When I try to share with you about the currents of feeling stirring in my belly, I feel the words get caught in my throat until I'm unable to speak.

I don't know you, but I love you,

Kamala

Getting close to someone, falling in love, and letting someone see you in all your pain and glory can be wildly terrifying. Inviting someone into your internal experience opens you up to being hurt. Expressing your feelings opens you up for someone else to shut you down.

It seems that if we don't share what is happening within, we can keep ourselves safe from being rejected or having someone use our own words against us. We actually put ourselves at a greater risk of being hurt if we don't express ourselves than if we do. If we keep our internal or emotional world buried and don't share, we push people away. If we want to be closer to another, we have to be willing to take risks and say the things we are most afraid to share.

Falling in love is a process of being vulnerable and letting go. Sometimes, when the heart opens wide, it's almost painful. The more we move into love, the more we have to let go. Falling in love can be terrifying because when we've found someone we delight in sharing ourselves with, we risk experiencing the pain of losing them. In order to open ourselves to love, we need to be willing to let go of the other person. The willingness to let go creates room for others to come closer. People can't move closer to us when we are right up against them. We can't receive the gifts we are being offered if our hands are busy clinging. When we practice owning our own desire without needing to change it or jump on it, we create more spaciousness. This gives us the freedom to come forward and the other room to move closer.

When we can just be with our desires, our desires don't have a hold on us. Our desires can be just what they are. They don't need to be chased or changed. They are alive and present in our body and there is nothing we need to do about it. When we are fully resting in our desire, without pushing it away or needing to act on it, it magnifies us rather than controls us. Embracing our own desires, the other won't feel the pressure of needing to fulfill our desires for us.

When we own our desires, we become filled by the desire itself. From this place, an invitation for intimacy or sex doesn't come from a sense of lack or need. Your desire becomes a gift that you share from a place of fulfillment. Embodied desires are invitations, seeking for what you can give rather than what they can get. As we embrace our desire, there is no rejection because we are fulfilled by desire itself. This type of expressed desire is rarely refused. When you exude your desire from your whole body, it's palpable and people will practically beg to fulfill this desire for you.

When you fully own your own desire, it really doesn't matter what someone else is or isn't doing. You are the only one in charge of your body. Owning your desire, you will be able to feel what is right for you and express exactly what you do and do not want. You call the shots on what you want to do and how you want to be touched. We can try to bypass what we feel, but then we become disjoined, frustrated, stuck, or confused."

Roadmap to Intimacy—Owning Your Desire

If you want to have pleasure in the bedroom, you have to create pleasure in your life. No one can give you the ecstasy you desire until you make friends with pleasure. Every day give yourself some kind of pleasure present or do something for yourself that reminds you that you are special.

1. Notice a desire you have right now. It may be simple like eating ice cream or it may be a deep yearning like being ravished by your partner.

2. Notice what happens in your body when you pay attention to the desire. You do not have to do anything about the desire. Don't judge it. Just notice what sensation your body feels when you are present with your desire.

3. Breathe into the desire. Feel it circulating through your whole body. Notice what it's like to just be with your desire without needing to change it or fulfill it. Notice what is pleasurable about the desire without even needing to do anything about it.

4. Slow down and let your whole body be filled by desire. What is the natural impulse you're experiencing? When you simply allow desire to circulate through your whole body, what happens when you let the desire move your body ever so slowly? Follow your body's natural impulse no matter how strange or simple it may be. Perhaps one finger starts to

move. Perhaps your mouth widens. Let the desire flood your body without needing to change it. Just let your body move ever so slowly as the desire swirls through you. Notice how sexy, alive, or present you feel as you embody your desire.

Saying What We're Afraid to Say

Dear Doyal,

Being with you is far lonelier than just being by myself. On my twenty-fifth birthday, I start crying, and don't stop for two months. I eat tears for breakfast, lunch, and dinner. I want you to wake up to see that I am beautiful and young and ready to be taken by your love.

We've been living in the woods together. I wanted to move in with you because you never called. Now that we're living together, you still never call. I wait for you to come home, and when you do, you're exhausted from your day of labor.

I try to engage you, but you grunt one-word answers. Late at night, when my sobs are too heavy to ignore, you finally scoop me up and bring your tenderness. And when the blankness of morning comes, the tears fall before I can even clean the crust from my eyes. I want you to tell me that you love me. I want you to tell me that you're overjoyed to be with me—to pull me close with passion and make me stop being afraid. But instead, you tell me you're in love with someone else because of how she sings, and you're not in love with me because I can't sing. There is a bomb strapped to my chest... Unsure when the inevitable explosion of heartbreak will strike.

I take singing lessons so you'll fall for me. If I sing sweetly enough, maybe you'll look at me the way you look at her. But I don't sing around you anymore.

I sing, "Dream a Little Dream" and try to get it perfect. I imagine the day that I will feel confident and bold enough to open my mouth and let the sounds spill out around you. But instead, when I open my mouth, black and silent birds fly out and fill up the space between us. I feel like I am being choked. The hands of the woman you're in love with are wrapped around my neck.

Instead of melodies, I sing to you with sobs,

Kamala

No one can take away your love.

There is no power in the universe to keep you from loving. No matter how trapped you might feel, you always have the freedom to love.

Even when someone else doesn't return or accept the love you are offering, they still cannot take away your love. Showing love can be terrifying. When we express it, we risk it being rejected. Few things are as painful as love not being received. Perhaps all pain stems from not giving or receiving enough love. When we are real and vulnerable with love, we have no idea how it will be met.

Loving and being loved are the most courageous acts, and are the gateways to connection and unity. It is easy to stay hidden behind defensive walls and not show we care. Sharing the things we are hiding and ashamed of can create shock waves that can leave us reeling to recover. Courage comes from opening to love. Letting it in and letting it be expressed fully. Real heroes don't run from love. Instead they open all the way and allow love to work through them.

Whenever we hold back from expressing ourselves, we create separation. To open to bold levels of honesty with others, we need to be radically honest with ourselves. We need to look within and ask ourselves at every turn what we are wanting, needing, and feeling. Holding back what is happening within doesn't keep us safe. All the things we don't say can fester inside and can send us farther from ourselves. Expressing ourselves can be scary, but the results of being unexpressed are far more frightening.

Being intimate requires us to be beyond courageous. Intimacy is not for the faint of heart. It requires us to seek truth on the deepest level of who we are and share that truth when we find it.

Roadmap to Intimacy—Uncovering What You're Afraid to Share

1. Get paper, pens, and a timer. For each writing prompt, keep your pen to the paper writing non-stop. Don't read it back. Don't edit it. Don't hold back.

2. For five minutes complete this statement:

   "What I'm afraid others won't love about me is…"

3. For five minutes complete this statement:

   "What I'm afraid others might find out about me is…"

4. For five minutes complete this statement:

   "What I'm afraid will ruin my life if it gets out is…"

5. Slowly read what you wrote back to yourself. Place a hand on your own heart and take deep breaths. Feel yourself loving the "worst" parts of you.

Being Completely Honest with Yourself

Dear Doyal,

In one week, I hear three people talk about the Vipassana ten-day meditation retreat. I've never been able to sit still for more than a few minutes at a time, but it's time to do something radically different. I make the long trip, crying the whole way, to sit in silent meditation for ten days. It's total bullshit and I want out as soon as I get here. We're not supposed to make eye contact or talk or write or exercise or do anything but sit, eat small meals, and sleep.

By the sixth day, I'm sure I won't make it to the end. I plot my escape. Bust into the office, get my car keys, and get the hell out of here. All we're doing is paying attention to our bodies and breath, and my body is where all the pain is. It hurts to be here. I can't stop crying, and so instead of meditating I go to my bunk and let my body be shaken by the tears.

I've felt so alone for so long. Why haven't you loved me? What will it take for you to see how amazing I am and for you to turn toward me? I've been desperate for your gentleness and love to replace all the pain of rejection.

Exhausted from crying, and suddenly, I feel the most loving, gentle, kind and tender touch I've ever felt. A hand slowly moves the hair out of my face and ever so softly wipes away the tears. As the hand brushes my hair back, I am aware of the immense light that is spilling into the room. Sunlight or God's light, I'm not sure, it seems like the same thing. I slowly look up to see what angelic creature has blessed me with the most loving touch I've ever felt. I study the hand as it moves in again to wipe away the last tear. Then I realize... it's my own hand. I feel my heart crack open so wide that the sunlight spills into my chest. How can my own hand touch me with such loving compassion?

I know that you'll never be able to touch me like this. All winter long I've wanted this kind of love from you. I know that no matter how much I try to get you to love me, it won't happen. I've been desperate for you to come closer, to be able to hold all my feelings, and listen to all the things I've been unable to speak. I am shaken by the love pulsing through me now. I love myself so much that I've come here to give me ten full days of undivided undistracted attention. I'm listening to all the things I've needed to say.

I've waited my whole life for a love like this,

Kamala

Often times we can't receive what we are desperate to get from others until we learn how to give it to ourselves. If we want to feel loved, special, and adored, we need to find ways to make ourselves feel that way. When we can fill ourselves up with the love we're wanting, we move out of desperation for someone else to give it to us.

If we want attention more than anything, we can find small ways to give it to ourselves everyday. That way, when others turn their attention away from us, we won't go hungry for attention. We can still want, need, and crave attention from others, but we are not desperate for it. Showing others we can give to ourselves removes pressure for others to be the sole provider for the attention we need. When we identify what we need and can give it to ourselves, we create opportunities for others to give more to us.

In order to be in-tune with our own needs, we need to be able to express ourselves. When we're expressing what we do and do not want, what we love and what we're feeling, we stop suppressing ourselves and create freedom to be who we are.

Often times we don't fully express ourselves, because we're ashamed of what we're feeling. Who wants to feel jealous, needy, greedy, resentful, or spiteful? These feelings can make us feel like we're terrible people. Most people don't want to express their feelings and thoughts because of the shame. We say to ourselves, "I shouldn't feel this way. I should just get over this. It is stupid to think like this."

We're all messy though. We all have issues. We all have ways we contract and we all have untrue stories we believe. The key isn't to bust through and cut out all the stories we've ever had. The key is to simply dissolve any shame we have by expressing what we're experiencing.

Expressing what we are feeling can help us to overcome the shames we have about how we are as human beings. Our unexpressed thoughts and feelings can ping-pong around inside of us until they are finally expressed. Unexpressed feelings will find a way to be heard. Suppressed feelings may come out as irrational anger, depression, mental fog, fatigue, sickness, cancer, violent thoughts; the list goes on. We are clever creatures. Jagged thoughts and feelings can become like slivers inside and our bodies will do whatever they can to get the sliver out.

Whatever we're feeling is okay. Maybe we want to rush through our feelings so we can feel good again. Or maybe we hold on to try and understand them. We don't need to examine where our feelings come from, why they're here, how long they're going to stay, when we are going to feel them again, who caused them, and why they caused them.

There is no need to create a story about why your feelings are here. You don't hold shit in your hand as it's coming out of your ass and examine it and hold onto it and complain about how bad it stinks. So why would we want to do that with our shitty emotions? When you take a shit you don't get mad at your partner for cooking tacos and making your poops smell bad. No, you get it out and you flush it down and it's gone. So why don't we do that emotionally? We don't need to churn the emotions over and over again hoping to make compost in our hands. That would take a long time and there are more fun things to do with our lives.

We can spend a lifetime in examination, but guess what? It doesn't bring us any closer to being intimate with others. What brings us closer to ourselves, to God, to our partners, to the beautiful magic that sparkles in each and every moment? What brings us closer is relaxing into our bodies and deciding that love is more important than our stories. Love is more important than our pain. Love is more important than holding onto what you think you are. If we want true intimacy we have to be ready to let each and every hurt and trigger in and out with a breath. Because we will get triggered. We will be hurt. We will wake up and feel like crap and possibly even feel like stabbing our partner. Guess what? That's okay. You are welcome to feel all of it.

When we acknowledge our feelings and express them, we can break out of cycles of opening up, getting hurt, and shutting down. It seems like emotions can turn us into morning glories where we open when the light of affection is shining on us and close when it's dark. One of the best ways to break the cycle of open and close is to stop trying to force ourselves out of what we are experiencing and share what is happening for us in this moment.

If we don't express our feelings and emotions, then we clench down on our consciousness and we stop expanding. You are the artist of your life. Your emotions are the paint for you to color your world. Don't block any of them off. The love, the joy, the pain, the murderousness—whatever is here, give space for it to be here. Create a pillowy room where you can invite whatever part of you is rising and say, "Welcome." Enwrap each part of you in your womb-like beingness.

The greatest gift we can give ourselves is to become a fully expressed, fully turned-on, intimately engaged human. This requires us to overcome the shame we have around our thoughts and feelings and be fully seen as who we are, in whatever form we're in.

Not who we pretend to be.

Not who we want to be.

Not who we think we should be.

Just who we are, moment by moment.

No matter how ugly, stupid, or fearful.

Whenever we feel ashamed about what we feel, we simply need to relax more deeply. We can take deep breaths and allow our bodies to relax. When we relax our bodies, we create space for ourselves to be here no matter how ugly or upset we might be in that moment.

Your ability to relax your body and shift your consciousness is not any harder than taking a breath. If you really want to change your world, take three deep breaths. Your body is amazing. It has the ability to calm down and create neurological and physiological changes with the magic bullet of the breath. I wish I could weave the sound of me breathing with you into the pages here because when more than one person breathes together, the potency of it increases exponentially. Our ability to shift our consciousness is truly only one breath away. It is not any more or less difficult than taking one single breath of intent.

In the practice of taking deep breaths and relaxing our bodies, we become conscious co-creators of our experience. We become empowered in every moment to dive deeper into ourselves and access whatever is there. This exercise expands our capacity to feel more of what lives in us, and it also allows us the freedom to let it go so we can make room for who we are without stories clouding our view.

We can't be who we have the potential to be when we haven't fully expressed who we are right now. When we acknowledge what we're feeling and speak up about what's going on, we can create opportunities to let it go.

We don't need to hold onto anything we're feeling because there will always be more emotions. Like everything, our emotions shift. Every emotion is in us at all times, and we all have emotions we tend to default toward. When we allow ourselves space to access more of our feelings, the less aversion or attachment we experience toward emotions, and the more full-spectrum we become.

Our feelings add richness and depth to the canvas of life. They are messages from within asking to be heard. When we hear them, feel them, express them and let them go, we can understand the messages they are sending us. With practice, feeling what we're feeling and letting it go, we will continue to find something new. It puts us in the driver's seat. This practice makes us the creator of our own lives and relationships in every moment. It allows us to let go of the tension of holding onto an experience. When we keep expressing and letting go, we stop being dictated by our shame about what we're feeling. We can empty out our contractions and be present to what we are experiencing.

Roadmap to Intimacy—Express and Move On

1. When you have something you want to share with someone, express what your intentions are for sharing with him or her. What do you really want? Do you want to feel closer or more connected them?

2. As you share, notice what you are feeling in your own body. What sensations are you aware of? What contractions or restrictions are you feeling? Share with the person.

3. Notice what is happening for you emotionally. Share what you are feeling. Keep it simple: sad, mad, or happy.

4. After you've shared your experience, let them know that you are sharing with them so you can let go of whatever you're feeling and move on. Say, "I'm letting you know so I can let this go."

6. Feel what is happening within you, and access your willingness to let it go. Take some deep breaths, make a sound, and shake your body. Make your process of letting go of what you shared palpable to the other person.

Your dialogue with the other person may sound something like this:

I want to feel _____ with you.
Example: I want to feel closer to you.

I am experiencing _____ in my body
Example: I am experiencing tension in my belly.

I feel _____right now.
Example: I feel scared right now.

I'm sharing this with you so I can let it go.

Love Magnet

Dear Doyal,

Since I've left you, I've been feeling alive again. We still sleep together, but it's just a casual every two week release. I only come to you now when I am too stressed to cope. Sleeping with you just treats the symptom of stress rather than addresses the root cause, but I still come to you. The moment I walked away from you, the pheromones of singleness flooded out of my body and have caused men to come flocking in. This is not unfamiliar, but this time I'm allowing myself to really delight in the lavishness of being doted on by many men.

You're the only one I'm making love with, but each night a new man comes to me with his praises and his passion. I am not dressing any differently. I am not announcing that I'm single. I am just simply walking through the world with buoyancy and a sense of being deeply committed to loving myself. Including you, I'm dating seven beautiful, brilliant, high-quality men, and turning away more. It's like the sky opened up and it is literally raining men.

The other morning as you walked out the back door, someone knocked on my front door. It was raining, and standing there in my doorway was a beautiful drenched dancer man that I haven't talked to or seen in months. As he stripped away his soaking clothes, he said he'd been walking since dawn to get to me—to confess his love.

All I could do was chuckle at the universe,

Kamala

When we are open, we are irresistible. When we are turned on and shining brightly within ourselves, we become magnets for love. We draw people in. This means we are fully engaging in whatever is present in the moment. We are tapped into our own bodies. It means we are alive and are acutely aware of the life-force pulsing through our own bodies. Our vision is clear and we feel inspired by the world around us.

It's not always easy to access and relax into our inner awesomeness. How can we move from life lacking luster to being tapped into the brilliance that pulses through all things? We can't force ourselves there. It requires us to be in-touch and in-love with whoever we are in this moment. Being in-tune with our own amazingness calls us to relax into ourselves.

When we are relaxed in our own bodies, others will relax around us. Our culture is relaxation deprived. We can be like spas that people can sink into. When you can encourage people to feel good, just with your being, they'll want more of what you've got. When you are vulnerable and transparent, people can relax even more around you. They won't have to question your motives. They'll know where you are coming from, and they will be able to breathe deeper around you.

When we can be present with other people's feelings, thoughts, and emotions, they will be drawn to us because, with us, they'll feel like they have a place to rest and fold into. We all want to be received. We all want to know that it is safe to open up. Our nervous systems can be on hyper-alert until a sense of safety is created. We want to know that if we open, we won't be judged or shamed for opening. When we hold a present and loving space for others, they'll know that they can relax and open around us.

Whatever people are bringing to us, we can ask ourselves, "How can I hold this? How can I open to this? How can I make more space for this person?" When someone is sharing something that is difficult for you to hear, feel into your own body. What pain or sensations are you aware of?

All your fears and pains are simply just body sensations, and your body sensations are always changing. So there is no need to run away from any of them. You don't have to be afraid of your sensations. When you simply breathe into them, you'll notice that they'll change. In fact, the only thing you can rely on is that they will change. When you are present within yourself, you can make space for anything others are bringing you. As you make space for them, they'll feel the deep restfulness of being accepted. They'll be hooked and keep coming back for more.

It is easy for others to fall in love with you. All it really requires is being present and not shrinking back. People want to feel met. This begins with something as simple as meeting someone's eyes and allowing yourself to simply gaze into them. It's making a connection and acknowledging that you are sharing the same space with others.

Being a magnet for love is about being so deeply present that the fabric of the world folds into you. You are sensually engaged with life, love, and understanding. Being a love magnet has way less to do with what you can gain and way more to do with what you can generate and give.

When you are radiantly alive, it is the sexiest most magnetic version of yourself you can be. When you are awake in your own skin, people will be drawn to that. People will be magnetically pulled toward you. It's not about gaining power over others, but inviting them in. Your magnetism has nothing to do with how seductive or pretty you are. It has everything to do with how fully you are opening—how you are showing up in the moment and being willing to turn on your own body.

Notice what it's like to be turned on by life.
Feel into your own aliveness.
Feel into your own brilliance.
Sensually engage with the world.
Reach out to meet people from this place.
Be fully plugged into who you are.

When we are relaxed in our bodies, a smile, eye contact, or a gentle touch is so much more than a curve of the lips or brush of fingertips. When we're in our bodies, our smile can radiate out every pore and wrap around the person we're engaging with.

People will feel lit up by our very presence. Being a magnet for love isn't about making people love us so we can feel better about ourselves. This is a superpower that anyone can have. When we show up in our bodies, turn on our love, people will be drawn to us.

When we deeply sink into ourselves, we make space for connection. In order to be beautiful magnificent magnets, we need to settle into ourselves, and relax our chests, bellies, and pelvises. Our legs can run away, our fists can punch, and our heads can create stories. When we let the edges of ourselves soften and relax the core of our bodies, we can give room for the most gifted parts of ourselves to bloom to the surface. Our hearts can breathe love, our bellies can hold our tenderness, and our pelvises can fill us with ecstatic pleasure.

As the light of who we are shines brighter, how do we deal with attracting the wrong kind of attention? Often people think they need to dim down in order to avoid drawing in the wrong kinds of people. When we are embodied, we don't have to shield ourselves. By being in our brilliance and connected to what we want, we don't attract the kind of people who will glom onto us. When we are dim, hiding our brightness, or checking out, people will see us as prey. When we are strong, rooted, and grounded in our radiance, we're not prey, we're king of the jungle.

Roadmap to Intimacy—Being a Love Magnet

1. Give yourself permission to take at least twenty minutes to relax into this exercise. Lay down on the earth or in a cozy room.

2. Take a deep breath, making a sound as you exhale. Breathe into your head and say the mantra, "I am alive."

3. Then, breathe deeply into your heart and say the mantra, "I am alive."

4. Breathe into your belly and say, "I am alive."

5. Breathe down into your pelvis and say, "I am alive."

6. Now breathe all the way down into your feet saying the mantra, "I am alive."

7. Feel the life-force pulsing through your whole body. Feel how you occupy yourself. Relax knowing there is nothing more you need to do, but be fully plugged into your own body in this moment. Feel into your ability to be penetrated by the universe and to penetrate the universe.

Expressing Anything and Everything

Dear Doyal,

It's good to leave things while they're good. Kauai has chewed me up and spit me out. This island seems to be rejecting us in the grossest ways possible.

You and I hear of an eleven-mile hike to a sacred valley. In my mind, it is heaven on earth. Naked women bathe in waterfalls, the trees are filled with over-ripe mangos and the ground is littered with ready to eat avocados. I think that somehow if we can make it into the Kalalau Valley, all our troubles will be washed away.

So determined to get there, I ignore the warnings of the countless deaths that have happened on this slippery trek. You nearly get washed away in the first mile crossing the violent river. The trail winds its way over steep dramatic cliffs that the ocean angrily pounds against. We hike on in the rain through burnt mud so slick that I keep falling on my ass until my pack and I are coated in the red thickness.

We don't say a word to each other. Not an, "I'm scared" or an "I think we should turn back."

I'm sure if we were speaking, we would have talked each other out of continuing. But somehow the deafening silence keeps us going with a brooding stubbornness. It isn't until I'm clinging on to the cliff's edge, clawing my way from death, that the dams of our voices finally break.

We're just a few miles from the valley. All that stands between paradise and us is this tiny slick trail with sheer cliffs falling forcefully below. We get to a section of the trail where there is no vegetation, just the impossibly slick mud and the jagged teeth of rocks opening to the mouth of the ocean. With overly confident steps I scoot myself backwards down the thin ledge while you hang back. Without warning, my legs slip out from under me. I fall face first into the thick mud. Panicked, I look for a root or rock or shrub to grab onto as I slide towards cliff's edge. There is nothing but mud.

I claw my fingers into the earthy goo and bury my knees and feet in as and try to gain traction. Behind me the edge is getting closer. It is here, with me looking into the face of death, where we finally start talking.

"I never wanted to come on this hike in the first place! Why would you fucking walk on that trail? You fucking bitch!"

I am more shocked by your screams then I am the promise of death that I am speeding toward. Somehow your freak out sends a wave of calm through my body. I assess the situation. With the heaviness of my pack, the steepness of the slope, and only the slip-and-slide of mud to grip to, I weigh the likeliness of me getting out of this situation alive.

"I told you we should have brought that rope. You said it would be too much weight. Why the fuck do I always listen to you?" Your screams continue.

Like trying to talk down a suicide jumper, I try to calm you. Don't worry. It's all going to be okay.

Is this how I'm going to die? With you yelling at me?

With my feet approaching the edge, I ever so slowly slide my hands through the mud upwards. I crawl towards safety one inch at a time. Two inches forward, one inch sliding back. It takes me twenty minutes to crawl ten feet back to the trail, you yelling at me the whole way. Covered in mud and exhausted from adrenaline, we decide to turn around. And even after the near death experience, I want to keep going. I want to be that valley.

This hike is so much like our relationship. An ideal of where we can get to while ignoring the warning signs the entire way. The walk back, all the things we never said to each other explode out of us. After two years of civilized silence, the venom spews from us at full wrath. It's so clear to me now that no matter how much I try to keep the peace, the unexpressed always finds a way to express itself.

We never make it to the valley,

Kamala

There are countless reasons to not speak up and share what we are thinking and feeling—fear of being rejected, shame about the way we feel, risk of being hurt, the list goes on. If we don't express what is happening within us, we're not being honest, authentic, and real about who we are. When we're holding back, what else are we doing but putting on a performance? When we don't express ourselves in our lives, our sex, our relationships, they become more about a performance than actually showing and sharing who we are.

As a general rule for intimacy—when we want to repress, it's time to express. The aspects of ourselves that we are afraid to share are the parts of us that most need to be seen. Where we are holding back is where we can access the keys to unlock the most gifted aspects of ourselves. If we want to feel deeply connected, we need to be willing to discover all the things we're not saying, and acknowledge or express them.

What would life be like if we weren't hiding out?

What would it be like if we were fully expressed?

Who are we kidding anyway?

Oftentimes we think we're not being seen, but people can see, feel, and know way more about us than we realize. All the things we don't say and the ways we hold back only push us away from ourselves and keep us separate from feeling love.

When we don't hide any part of who we are, we become more accessible and congruent. When we draw together all the aspects of ourselves that are floating around or buried within we create a solid message of who we are. The more we express all the different aspects of ourselves, our fears, joys, shames, vulnerabilities, the more we free up energy and tap into our passions and purpose for life.

Roadmap to Intimacy—Express Anything and Everything

1. With your journal or with a partner, start breathing deeply into your belly.

2. If you're alone, place a hand on your belly. If you're with a partner, place a hand on each other's bellies and encourage your breath to move each other's hands.

3. Write or share, "What I am afraid to share is…"

4. Share as much as you can while maintaining deep belly breaths.

♥ Find people you trust who you can share the parts of yourself you're afraid to show. Sometimes talking with someone, other than your partner, can help you see and realize things you normally wouldn't. Consider working with a coach who can be a guide for you: www.kamalachambers.com

Summary & Quotes to Share

Intimacy requires us to be radically honest. By expressing what is happening within, moment-by-moment, we dissolve our shames, connect deeper, and become magnets for love.

Inviting Others In

✤ If we want to be closer to another, we have to be willing to take risks and say the things we are most afraid to share.

✤ When we are fully resting in our desire, without pushing it away or needing to act on it, it magnifies us rather than controls us.

✤ When we are fully within our desire, there is no rejection because we are fulfilled by desire itself.

Saying What We're Afraid to Say

✤ Loving and being loved are the most courageous acts, and are the gateways to connection and unity.

✤ Whenever we hold back from expressing ourselves, we create separation.

✤ Intimacy requires us to seek truth on the deepest levels of who we are and share that truth when we find it.

Being Completely Honest with Yourself

❄ Often times we can't receive what we are desperate to get from others until we learn how to give it to ourselves.

❄ When we're expressing what we do and do not want, what we love and what we're feeling, we stop suppressing ourselves and create freedom to be who we are.

❄ Expressing what we are feeling can help us to overcome the shames we have about who we are.

Love Magnet

❄ Being in-tune with our own amazingness calls us to relax into ourselves.

❄ When we can be present with other people's feelings, thoughts, and emotions, they will be drawn to us because they'll feel like they can rest and fold into us.

❄ Your magnetism has nothing to do with how seductive or pretty you are. It has everything to do with how fully you are opening and showing up in the moment.

Expressing Anything and Everything

❧ When we don't express ourselves, our relationships become more about performance than actually sharing who we are.

❧ The aspects of ourselves that we are afraid to share are the parts of us that most need to be seen.

❧ The more we express all the different aspects of ourselves, our fears, joys, shames, vulnerabilities, the more we free up energy and tap into our passions and purpose for life.

✉ Share on Facebook and Tweet @KamalaChambers

SIX

DARIUS

Facing Shadows and Igniting Passion

When I met Darius, I was suspicious of him. But because he was a teacher and practitioner of Energy Medicine like me, I felt met by him in ways I'd never experienced before. I didn't trust him, I wanted to keep him at a distance, but when someone I deeply cared for got sick, I didn't have the fight in me to keep Darius's pursuits at bay.

If narcissism and codependence made a baby, it would look like the ugly beast of our relationship. With Darius, my shadows were out-of-control. Being with someone who I had a sense was a spiritual con artist, aggravated my already present self-judgments. Because some of the profound sexual and spiritual experiences we had together, I was willing to be tossed around in the washing machine of the relationship.

After two years together, without explanation, Darius abruptly ended our relationship and cut off all communication between us. I was left battling my stories of the reasons why he left.

Through the letters in this chapter, I hope you'll be able to relate to my story and avoid falling into similar traps. May the lessons and roadmaps be a guide for you as you navigate your way through self-judgments, stories, and shadows. In the following pages, you're invited to bring all of yourself forward, no matter how "ugly" you believe that part of you to be. When we stop hiding away the parts of ourselves that we don't want others to see, we make room for fun and passion to fill us up again.

Inviting All of Yourself Forward

Dear Darius,

We meet on a rooftop.

Without knocking, I open the doors timidly to what I believed to be some kind of swinger sex party. I have no idea what I am getting into. To my relief the house is vacant. There are no sex swings in the living room or men with hard-ons ready to pounce. I follow a trail and a murmur of laughter to the backyard and find a ladder; I assume to climb. On the roof is a long pile of people wrapped in each other's arms.

The sun is setting and a full moon is rising. There in the pile of bodies is my beautiful friend Peter, the only person I know. I fall into his arms giggling, and press my body against him and you. A dark haired woman cradles you, thin and pretty. Peter introduces you as a fellow Energy Medicine teacher.

You and I look into one another for the first time. The darkness of your eyes matches your complexion. I study your mischievous nose and wonder if you're attractive. Sleep crusts to the corner of your eyelashes and I decide you don't take care of yourself. Suspicion distorts both our faces.

It's not often we meet other Energy Medicine teachers. I pull on my coat of importance. We brag back and forth about the depth of the curriculum we both teach.

As we talk, I cuddle into you more. The woman you're with confuses me with looks of welcoming me closer to you. I am certain you're lovers, and her total openness to the interest brewing between us is unfamiliar. I have never felt such a lack of threat from a woman.

I lean my head into your chest, and breathe you in. The first inhalation of you is intoxicating. Inhaling your heart I start giggling and feel like a stoner taking a bong rip. Breathing in your heart somehow feels as though it's as pure and loving as the heart of Jesus. I put my lips to your heart chakra again and take a drag, smoking the pink mist of your heart's love. You move into my lungs and swirl inside, getting me high.

I've always felt like my heart is inaccessible and vile. After experiencing a heart like yours, I want more.

High on you,

Kamala

Each one of us has a garden inside. The purpose of intimacy is nourishing that garden and exploring the garden inside another. Accessing these gardens has nothing to do with chanting or burning incense or being what the other wants us to be. It has everything to do with our imperfections. Our imperfections are actually the compost that help our inner gardens grow.

We may want a perfect garden growing within, with no weeds of jealousy, fear, doubt, or anger crowding out who we know we can be. We can hate the garden for not being perfect, but the only way we have power to change our internal landscape is by accepting it, tending to it, and finding the miracles buried in it. What is one person's weed is another person's medicine. Just because you don't want the weeds to be there doesn't make them bad. Most people want to rid their yards of dandelions, while others use them as a powerful digestion tonic.

When we are attentive to our internal garden, who we're trying to be dissolves. We can arrive at who we actually are in this moment. Tending to our own pains and imperfections, and holding our own inadequacies allows us to unlock the key to our original essence. We relax deeper, expand, and let the gates to the internal garden open when we can nurture the hurt parts of ourselves and be present with our own shortcomings. There is never an end to the weeds of our issues. Gardens are always growing. And it is with our attention, care, and nurturing that we can make space for our flowery gifts to blossom.

By accessing our internal landscape, we experience more in every moment. When we are tending our own inner gardens, we create spaciousness to intimately explore the gardens of others. When we explore others and ourselves as though we are discovering a secret garden, we can wake up a deep appreciation for what each interaction offers. When we stroll through gardens with appreciation, we can dip into the wonders of what each weed of judgment and flower of passion is offering. Our weeds will show us exactly where we can accept ourselves. Our flowers will show us our brilliance. When we appreciate every aspect of the garden, we can access the medicine of every weed and the miracle of every flower.

Roadmap to Intimacy—Exploring Your Inner Garden

1. Imagine every aspect of you is a plant in a garden. Your emotions, your thoughts, your feelings…all are aspects of the beautiful garden that is you.

2. What are the inner flowers of yourself that you love most? Make a list or share with a partner all the aspects of yourself that you love most.

3. What do you consider as your inner weeds? What is crowding out the parts of you that you want to flourish? Now share what your weeds are. What are the things that strangle out the parts of you that you love most?

4. If we just try to rip out the weeds, we won't get the whole root and they keep growing back. Dissolving our issues, at the root level, requires mindfulness. Meditate on your inner weeds. Notice how your body feels when you bring them to mind. Breathe into how those weeds are living in your body. Without trying to change them or run away from the discomfort of them, just notice what is there.

5. Notice how your inner flowers are living in your body. Breathe into the areas of your body where you feel the flowers of you are blooming. Follow the pleasure of experiencing the greatest aspects of you flourishing in your own body.

6. Share with your journal or with a partner what you noticed. Continue to practice, noticing how the weeds of your personality show up in your body

without trying to change them. Notice what it's like for the flowers of what you love most about yourself to be shined on by the sun of your attention.

The Shadow - Can I Love This Too?

Dear Darius,

I feel like I'm watching a car crash, and don't know where the brakes are or how to stop it. Falling in love with you seems like the worst thing I could do, but you're persistent and have some kind of inescapable hold on me. It's like you shape shift into exactly who I need you to be.

My last relationship was with a man who ignored me and said he could never love me. The experience of not being loved fits into my image. It fits into my childhood stories. Being loved 100% of the time, like a spotlight perpetually beaming on me, is terrifying.

Now, you're showing up and promising that kind of love. All my old ideas of not being good enough have to die and they are fighting to live. In the face of this much love, I hate myself. In this much light, shadows fight to live. I show you my ugly, and the act of exposing it somehow makes it beautiful.

You come up from Seattle to visit me in the island mansion I'm living in. My friend Kevin shows up. I'm excited to introduce you two, but Kevin is consumed with darkness. He seems like a shell of his normal self. Next to the light of your beautiful heart, his darkness seems blinding. He talks about how his girlfriend had an abortion and he's been feeling a pain in his chest ever since. He believes that the spirit of the child is living in his chest, and that it's his responsibility to keep it safe. You and I look at each other knowingly. We both see clearly that it's not the spirit of the child, but an entity that is feeding off Kevin.

With Kevin's permission, you and I go to work on removing the demonic force. Soon into the process, we both realize this is one of the darkest, slimiest, most terrifying creatures either of us has ever encountered. It seems more than we can handle. You get out a dagger made of selenite and chant invocations. I try to remove the entity the ways I know how, but nothing works. I can tell the only thing that will get this deeply rooted entity out of Kevin's body is to give it a new host.

I think about the movie The Exorcist, when the priest takes the demon into his own body. I think it's the only way, and I trust that once it's in me I can get rid of it without having to jump out a window. With all the light and power I can draw in, I suck the creature out of Kevin and instantly feel it wrap around me like an octopus.

I hear a slow, low demonic laughter. I look around the room to see where it is coming from. You and Kevin look at me, unblinking, and it takes me longer than it should to realize the sound is coming from me. I break away from you and move toward the door. I want to get this thing out of the house. It's hard to move my body. I can already feel its energy slithering into me. I make my way to the lawn and it knocks me to my knees. The crazed unfamiliar cackle still rumbling from within. I wrestle with my own body trying to expel the entity that is trying to take me over. It grabs ahold of my own hands, and they claw at my throat trying to strangle me.

I breathe and focus on raising my vibration so high that there is no way this low vibration can live in me. With an eerie screech, it jumps out of my throat and out of my body. I lay on the grass panting.

That was stupid of me. I chuckle to myself. By the time I get back to the house, Kevin feels like himself again and I have a large blister starting to fester on my mouth. You grab my face and point your dagger inches from my lips. With the intensity of an evangelical preacher you chant invocations that I don't understand until I'm dry heaving on the floor.

When it's all over, we look at one another exhausted. This will be just the first of many dramatic energetic experiences we have together, equally as terrifying and exhilarating. Again and again you and I are faced with darkness, both our own and outside influences. Again and again we are tested to rise up into higher states of love.

When we can't find love, we become overrun by the darkness,

Kamala

The shadow refers to all the things we want to keep hidden—the parts of ourselves that we are ashamed of and fear. We keep these parts hidden because of fear that if people knew this part of us, surely they would reject us. The common fear is if people knew the shadows lurking within, they would see us as unlovable.

Our shadows seem like the aspects of ourselves we need to get rid of, but our shadows can be our greatest allies. We keep the shadow hidden and protected so we can stay protected. If we really want intimacy, the shadow needs to be brought into the light. To make this happen, we need to be willing to look at, show, and learn to love all the parts of ourselves we've kept hidden.

In order for us to experience true intimacy, we must be completely honest and present with all of who we are. This means not rejecting any part of ourselves no matter how ugly, vile, or beautiful it may be. Intimacy with another doesn't happen by overriding any part of ourselves. Intimacy requires vulnerability that takes an awesome courage to find.

When we withhold the shadows about ourselves, we create tension and a sense of separation. When we try to suppress our shadows, they don't go away, they just find other ways of expressing themselves. Our unexpressed shadows may come out through depression, irrational anger, mistrust—the list goes on. When we share our shadows with others, it can be like lacerating a boil. Willingness to open ourselves to another and express our shadows relieves the depression, anger, and mistrust. We can courageously move through the world and make the choice to not hold back. We make the choice to be completely honest.

When we make the choice to be completely honest, others will feel more relaxed around us. People are way more intuitive than we give them credit for. Others are continually responding to our unexpressed feelings, emotions and thoughts. We are not isolated beings. Everything that goes on internally affects the outer world. If we want people to trust us, we must be willing to be completely transparent.

Oftentimes, we think we need to trust people first in order to be transparent with them. If we lead with trying to figure out if someone is trustworthy, we have the expectation that they are going to hurt us, and ultimately they'll oblige. If we expose ourselves and someone sees who we really are, we risk being hurt even more.

Our vulnerability is NOT dangerous when we lovingly and compassionately hold ourselves. It can be terrifying to be vulnerable because we've all been hurt. Vulnerability owns our ability to feel. Intimacy is carried on the wings of our courage to express what we're feeling. Vulnerability is courageous, not weak. When we are present with ourselves, we say "I am going to be here for me no matter what," and then no one has the power to hurt us.

Lead with the determination to be present with your self.

Lead knowing you have your back no matter what.

Lead with the truth that the only way to really trust someone is to be completely honest.

No one can ever hurt us when we lead with the shadow. When we are holding ourselves with love and without judgment, it really doesn't matter how someone responds to our vulnerability.

Being real, open, and honest are the best ways to love ourselves. I'm going to let you in on a little secret, your vulnerability can be the sexiest thing about you. When we are willing to show what is real and what is going on inside, people trust us more. Vulnerability invites people into our internal world. When we share, people don't have to be left guessing what we're feeling, what we're thinking, or what we're going to do next. They can relax and open and almost instantly feel closer to us. Our vulnerability creates a sense of trust.

We don't have to worry if it is safe for us to be vulnerable. No one is trustworthy, but everyone is worth our trust. We can trust that people are going to behave exactly as they do. When people do things that hurt us, they are acting outside of the story we told ourselves about who we think they are. We get angry because they are not behaving according to the story we made up about them. When we stop making up stories about others, they won't hurt us.

When we decide to be vulnerable and to stop feeding the stories we have about others, we see that there is really no separation between us and everything else. It is the idea of separation that creates disconnect. When we consciously decide to vulnerably show our shadows, we acknowledge that there is really no separation and we are everything.

Roadmap to Intimacy—Five Ways to be More Vulnerable

1. Ask for Help

   Intimacy is begging you to be willing to receive.

2. Share How You Feel

   Intimacy needs your expression and urges you to not hold back. Share your fears and joys and sensations that are happening in the moment.

3. Relax Your Body

   How can others relax and sink in with you when you are tense? Put a hand on your belly and take deep breaths until you fully relax.

4. Move Physically Closer

   When you are feeling contracted or scared someone doesn't love you or accept you, courageously reach out and gently touch the person you are backing away from.

5. Be Radically Honest

   Whatever you don't want to say, share it. Let people know what you really think.

Making Space For All of You

Dear Darius,

Tom, the man I've been caring for the past seven years is sick, like really sick. Cancer. He just got into bed one day, and he hasn't gotten up. I know I can't split my time between the island where I live and visiting you in Seattle anymore.

You come up to the island, and despite me telling you I don't want you to live with me, you don't leave. I don't even know you, and I don't have the energy or the time to try and get to know you. I haven't met your friends. I don't know where you've been or where you want to go. When you tell me stories about your past, I can't shake the feeling that you're lying to me. Getting into a new relationship requires time and energy that I don't have right now.

My whole life has become about caring for Tom. It has all just happened so quickly. Every day, I see him deteriorate, and I feel the weightiness of being a caregiver to someone I don't know how to help.

I hire a team to help me and end up fighting with them all to support the ever-changing alternative medicine treatments that his wife is desperate for him to try. She keeps shelling out *buckets of his money trying to find the magic bullet to get him to bounce back. You have these grandiose ideas of what's going to heal him. You preach until she gives you $10,000 to help her. As soon as it's clear that this is a situation beyond repair, you lose interest. Either that or you got your money so you're done. I don't know. I'm too flooded to try and figure you out right now.*

I'm working with doctors all over the world trying to implement the latest and greatest alternative medicine treatments. Instead of getting better, Tom just gets skinnier, weaker, and more incoherent.

Tom doesn't want to be here anymore, yet I feel responsible for keeping him alive. The team of caregivers are trying to help him die and the people who love him are desperate for me to do more to keep him alive. I am at war with myself. He doesn't want to be here. I can feel his spirit begging to be let go and yet all the treatments I implement just prolong the agony.

A month before Tom dies, he calls me into his room. It smells like death and I've been avoiding coming in here. It is too painful to see this 6'4" man that I care for so deeply wasted down to sixty-five pounds. His ankles are skinnier than my wrists. He tells me he doesn't want me here anymore. He hasn't been happy that you've moved in, and that his wife is giving you money for treatments you're not doing. He tells me you and I have two weeks to move out and he doesn't want me to come back. I try to talk to him, but he turns his head away in finality. How can I argue with a dying man? I have no more fight left in me. It's the last time I see Tom before he dies. We spent seven years together, me supporting him through health, holidays, his wedding, his dying, and this is how it ends.

I am beyond devastated. As soon as Tom asks us to leave the mansion you moved into with me, you tell me you cheated on me and break up with me. Suddenly I've lost you, my job, my house, my family I created with Tom and his wife. I want to believe that you're not leaving because you have nothing left to take from me. I want to believe that you are more than a spiritual con-artist.

Now that I need you, you're gone,

Kamala

Our western culture is flooded with disconnection. Even many "spiritual" people seem radically disconnected from themselves and others. When we are disconnected it's hard to discern what's best for us, and it's even harder to give voice to the parts of ourselves that intuitively know best.

When we are not intimately connected to ourselves, it's hard to know if our connection with another is genuine. Creating intimacy takes self-honesty, and it requires us to show up in the world with a willingness to be vulnerable.

Creating this type of intimacy with ourselves is radical. The last person our culture tells us to listen to is ourselves— our own hearts and our own intuition. Yet, it's crucial we stay tuned in to ourselves. We must be willing to see all the parts of ourselves that are not always so pretty, so clear, or so visible. This journey of self-discovery is like going snorkeling in the murky ocean looking for gems— it's difficult but if you look you'll find the most precious stones of all.

Are you willing to love yourself despite what you find?

Can you be here for the parts of you that are ugly and the parts of you that are beautiful?

Are you willing to be brave enough to look at the shadow, AND show your shadows to others?

Roadmap to Intimacy—Making Space for All of You

1. Spend some time stretching your body so you feel like you can rest comfortably in yourself.

2. With yourself or with a partner, take three deep breaths, making a sound as you exhale. If you're working with a partner, make eye contact during the whole exercise and switch roles after the first person is done sharing.

3. Share with your partner or a journal:

> I am afraid you will not love me because…
>
> What I am afraid for you to know about me is...
>
> What I judge about you/others is...
>
> I can't believe I'm going to tell you...
>
> One thing I love about you/others...
>
> One thing I admire about you/others…

4. After each share, go slowly, and take a deep breath. Notice how sharing feels in your body.

5. Share how that experience was for you.

Delighting in Love Again

Dear Darius,

I'm on a black sand beach, on the island of Ometepe, in the middle of Lake Nicaragua between two volcanoes. I came to Nicaragua alone and on a whim. A place my finger landed on a spinning globe. I bought my ticket because I needed a scene change. I didn't have my house or job or even you. It seemed coming to a place I knew nothing about would help me unpack the devastation of the past year with you. The day I landed, I found out Tom crossed over. He died and I wasn't there.

After I bought my ticket here, you decided you still wanted to be with me. You've come up with this grandiose idea of opening a retreat center, and I think you want me to fund it.

I am happy to be here without anyone I know, in a country that wants nothing from me, rich with a language I do not speak—a palate cleanser to the intensity of our experiences. You're mad at me for being here and not back there taking care of you. It's like I've been tangled up with you, and it feels good to slowly start to feel who I am without you pulling my strings.

Even when I am free and light, you have a way of worming your way through me that I can't seem to shake. I've found a group of four men to travel with here. All of us solo travelers came together to make our experiences a little richer.

The boys are out for a swim right now and I opted for the shore. Something in these lone moments carries nostalgia, a sort of soft gentle sadness with no cause or purpose. I flip through the overstuffed book of our memories together and wonder once again how I got here and really what this trip is about. So far it's been about having courage and breaking the mold of life as I knew it. It's been about fun, which before seemed to be a petty motivation. But now it feels like one of the most important tasks I can take on.

The boys and I climbed a volcano straight up yesterday. On the descent, my legs stopped following my mind. I asked them to move forward and my knees would buckle randomly. I asked them to hold my weight and they would collapse underneath me. The trail was a rocky riverbed, so steep that if filled with water it would be falling rather than flowing. The vertical descent was not a place for unmoving legs. What saved me were the hands of my fellow travelers.

When I had their hands, I became stable enough to continue the trek. When they let go, I became wobbly like Bambi's first steps. I couldn't comprehend why my legs decided to quit. "We've gone far enough," they screamed and without pain they became two wobbling sticks that would buckle without warning. The *four men and I all danced down the mountain together. When I needed their hands, they were there. I have felt more safe and cared for by these strangers than I have ever felt with you.*

Walking the dirt streets and on the mountain with them, I feel protected. I am not treated delicately but with respect. I am happy to be in this position to receive and to be a woman walking in the protected circle of these men. With you, it's been more about what you can get rather than what you can give.

Falling in love with my life again,

Kamala

Sometimes taking a pause is the best way to gain clarity. When we are immersed and saturated in the thickness of a situation, the best thing to do is step away to get clarity and perspective and have a chance to really hear what our intuitive wisdom has to say. In relationships, it's easy to get constricted around the patterns we repeat with our partners. How can we see ourselves or the other person for who they are when we're pressed right up against them?

We all need opportunities to step back, gain clarity, and see a bigger picture. This requires us to take breaks from our mundane ways of being and do something that delights us. We don't have to do things that push others away, but we can simply take breaks that encourage more fun and play. We can even invite our partners along for the fun.

Everything is constantly changing and the universe is in constant flux. In order for us to not fight against the nature of existence, we need to be willing to flux too. Every moment is new, with something new always being expressed. When we don't make up our minds about "the way things are" and meet the world with curiosity in every moment, we get to meet each moment with presence. When we stay curious, our partners will have the opportunity to continually surprise us.

Each breath becomes an opportunity to fall in love again. Every time we make love, we can bring something new. Since everything is constantly changing, there is really no need to hold onto a certain way of being. We don't even need to hold onto pleasure. In the next moment, pleasure may return, but it is the loss of attachment to it that keeps it new, fresh and ever present.

When we are creating stories about ourselves or our partner, then we step out of the delightful experience of discovering who someone is in this moment. We can't just eradicate all our stories at once, but what we can do is keep taking pauses and asking ourselves moment-by-moment, "Is this true? Is what I am thinking and feeling directly related to what I am actually experiencing in this moment?"

Roadmap to Intimacy—Let Go of What Was and Discover What Is

♥ Journal about what untrue stories are playing in your mind about yourself and your partner. What truth would you rather be living? If these stories are holding you back, write them out, and burn them with the intention of moving on.

♥ On a cellular level, we are all constantly changing. Who you were a week ago is not who you are today. Appreciate every moment with your beloved as though these are your first moments together.

♥ When you kiss, do it as though you've never tasted lips before. When you touch, explore as though you've never touched skin before. When we are curiously engaged with our partners, it calls us to be fully present with the magic of the moment.

Self-Judgment

Dear Darius,

    I started an intensive Tantra training with a group of women today. The first thing we do, before any niceties, is one by one strip off our clothes and step naked into the center of the circle. Each woman takes her time to introduce what she loves and hates about her body. As I study the many shapes and textures of the women, I am in awe of how beautiful each unique body is.

    Each woman scrutinizes herself against impossible standards. The stories from the women who introduce their beautiful, self-judging bodies are burned into me now. I grew up being told that women are backstabbing bitches. Standing naked in the middle of a circle of these scary creatures, I introduce them to my body with hot tears and a shaky voice. They stare at me—my flaws, my folds of fear, my shames uncovered. They love me, and I hate them for it. I rejoin the circle and become one of those expectant onlookers. One after another, each woman takes her place in the center—naked and afraid. Telling her own story of her ugliness. I can't comprehend their self-hatred. How could these incredible beings of soft folds and tender skin be so blind to their own magnificence? With each share, I melt more. I love them deeper. It seems every woman carries lies about her body. And if they are all this beautiful but can't see it, then I must be too.

I think of how you've explored the entire landscape of my body and loved it. Your ability to embrace all of my "flaws" has glued me to you. I want to make a confession to you. A secret I've gone to great lengths to hide. One that has destroyed relationships and has been a steel trap on my heart: I've hated myself more than I've ever hated anyone. I grew up as the runt in a pack of wolves. Because I wasn't fast enough, strong enough, smart enough to win love or keep pain away, I despised myself. I've strived to achieve and somehow out-race my inner "vile hideous evilness."

I've been thinking a lot about civil rights lately. I feel sick over how people are treated and abused because of their race, gender, and sexual orientation. I just want to pick up the world and shake all the hatred and fear out. I'm baffled by hatred and yet I've been a breeding ground for it.

I am sorry for contributing to the hatred in this world. For today, I am taking a stand in the best way I know how. From my heart, body, and soul I am making a promise to you. I promise to recognize that hatred is the heart crying to be shared. I promise that no matter how much or little I achieve in this life, I will love myself. I promise to stop wasting precious energy on self-judgment and instead use that energy to spread love.

Are you up for a revolution that begins with self-acceptance?

Kamala

Intimacy invites us to love each part of who we are. The ugly and the beautiful. As we are able to connect and love the many facets of ourselves, we're able to experience more connection with the many facets of others. When we stop trying to hide the parts of ourselves that we don't like, the more we'll feel integrated and complete.

Do you find yourself depleted of energy?

Do you sometimes judge others or put yourself down?

Do you have trouble making decisions or feeling excited about life?

Do you keep looking for fulfillment in relationships and meaningful experiences, but nothing works?

If you answered, "yes" to ANY of these questions, it's likely that you're suffering from self-judgment. Yeah, yeah. We all know we need to love ourselves. Self-love is one of the most basic things we should have learned in kindergarten, right? Not all of us did.

The relationship between you and yourself is the only relationship that lasts an entire lifetime and stays with you always. Yet, the self too often becomes overridden. Self-judgment is a slippery snake that can subtly worm its way through, eating away at your relationships and self-esteem. Quietly echoing an undercurrent of,

"You're not good enough."

"No one will ever fully love you."

"Why even try?"

Self-judgment is a silent relationship killer. It can affect us in more ways than we even realize. Self-love is the oxygen for living a passionate life.

Lacking in self-love often:

-Fuels the patterns of shutting down and lashing out
   in our relationships.
-Keeps us hungry and reaching for the next snack,
   movie, or sexual experience.
-Holds us back from grabbing hold of our own
   precious life and passionately creating it the way
   we want it to be.

How can we create peace in our relationships when we're busy attacking ourselves? Self-acceptance is revolutionary, and opens new pathways to have a wild love affair that lasts a life-time.

When you love yourself, you'll feel confident, and confidence is the sexiest of all character traits. Consider what makes you feel feminine or masculine, and get in touch with it. You can find great power and confidence when you radiate your femininity or masculinity. To keep your confidence strong, incorporate activities into your day that recharge your feminine or masculine qualities.

Roadmap to Intimacy—Naked Self

1. To deepen your self-acceptance, try this exercise. Get naked in front of a partner or a mirror and stand back. Introduce your body to your partner or yourself.

2. Share all the things you do and do not love about your body.

3. Breathe deeply and end by sharing the top five things you love most about your body.

Igniting Passion

Dear Darius,

We dive full on into the mystery.

We spend the weekend in the forest immersed in Tantra with a half dozen other couples. You and I explore worlds, and we make love that changes me to the core. We energetically meet each other and keep calling one another to open more.

We make love in a room filled with other couples making love. You spend lifetimes inside me. I become Kali and still you keep loving me. I become a goddess, a beast, a jester, a saint, a murderer, and still you keep loving me. Your love moves into every cell of my body until I undeniably see that everything I've been reaching for in you is alive in me. All my vileness and all my beauty is equally welcomed and embraced and important.

This experience feels like the climax of us and I don't know what happens. You shut down. You stop communicating. You stop making love with me. I try to pull you out, but I don't know how. Maybe we opened too much? Maybe you can't handle the amount of love we broke into?

For half a year, you seem like a shell of the man I loved. I feel like I'm in a sexless prison. You only turn toward me when it's painfully obvious that you want something from me. I don't know how to navigate the sea of undiagnosed disorders you seem to be suffering from. But the depth of that experience, of being so energetically matched by you, keeps me holding on. It keeps me hungry and hopeful that we'll get there again.

What will it take to have depth with you again?

Kamala

Making love can be a doorway to uncovering important aspects of who we are, where we stand naked and undefended in the presence of love and acceptance. Making love can invite us to transcend beyond average sex into a world of the most loving experiences of our lives.

To experience profound levels of pleasure and presence with another, we must slow down, breathe, and give our bodies a chance to feel all the subtle and sensuous sensations it's capable of. Pleasure becomes easy when we soften the edges of ourselves - our arms and legs. We can explore how effortless we can make our breathing. Our bellies and chests can be like balloons expanding and deflating, but when we breathe into the balloon, there is a certain amount of force to get the balloon of our chests to expand and contract.

There is a deeper practice to breathing. We can expand our breath to every part of our bodies. When we let our breath softly flow to every cell, it creates an organic and deeply intimate experience with ourselves.

Let your breath curl its way to your limbs.
Move out of the struggle to deepen your breath.
Let your body be breathed.

When we let our bodies be breathed, we become acutely aware of the sensuousness of life, of the perfumed petals of a flower, of the tickle of our fingertips on our own face, of the soft folds of flavor as we bite into a mango.

From this place, we embrace and are turned on by all that life is bringing us. Being turned on by life awakens profound levels of awareness, pleasure, and passion in the bedroom.

Roadmaps to Intimacy—Making Love with Awareness

Before you make love:

♥ Make sure that before you enter any lovemaking experience, you feel whole and complete, and are not just making love because you feel like something is missing. When you approach lovemaking from a place of desperation, you risk feeling more desperate than before.

Lovemaking is not a way to fulfill something that is lacking. It is a way to enhance what is already there. It can take a blissful bond and make it even richer.

♥ Create a safe space where you can both relax and be centered in the moment. When you touch, do it as though your hands are made of love, as though the area of the body you are contacting is a sacred artifact, as though you've never seen anything as beautiful as the being before you, as though you are exploring the very essence of your partner.

♥ Create opportunities to physically connect without moving into foreplay. Non-agenda touch can help build a sense of safety together, which is essential for connected loving. Spend time cuddling, dancing, and massaging one another with no agenda for sex.

♥ Flirt with your lover and build sexual energy without having sex right away. Out of this "prolonged turn on" you can feel truly alive. Sexual energy is creative energy, so stay turned on all day and get stuff done!

❤ Before touching your lover, do the following exercise: clap your hands together once and then rub them together vigorously for a few seconds.

❤ Using fingertips, trace slow "tingle" circles on your palms. See if you can extend this tingle sensation to your forearms. Now try it on your lover's palms.

❤ Your lover's pelvis and perineum have nerve pathways, that when massaged, can increase sexual pleasure. Lovingly massage and hold tender points for a minute or more and then move to the next point, making a circle around perineum and pelvic floor. One receives and one gives and then switch. Start with five minutes each.

While you're making love:

❤ Make eye contact. Breathe together. Check in with one another. Read each other's bodies. Let your sounds tell your partner how you're feeling.

❤ Go spelunking in your lover's eyes and seek the divine spark inside of them. Practice recognizing the aspect of them that is God/Spirit/Cosmic Energy.

❤ Rather than being motivated by orgasm, keep your attention on love. If things get too exciting and you lose the focus of love, then slow down, breathe, and bring it back to your heart. Bring your focus back to a loving space rather than ravaging desire.

Passion is not about how hot you can get or what positions you can contort into. Passion is about heart connection. It's about how deeply you can connect to your partner.

♥ The sounds you make invite your partner into your experience. Let your sounds tell your partner how you're feeling.

You don't have to scream your vocal cords mute to get your point across either. Simple moans, sighs, and sweet tones can clue your partner in to how you're feeling and what you're experiencing.

♥ Breathe together. Check in with one another. Read each other's bodies.

♥ Become effortless lovers! While you are pleasuring one another, breathe in deeply and slowly until you are "relaxed-while-aroused." Touch the edge of orgasm seven times or until your limbs and body feels weightless and float and move without effort. Let your divine "arousal energy" move you!

After you make love:

♥ Foreplay, mid-play, and after-play are all equally important. Spend time in a loving embrace with your partner. Even after your movement has stopped, keep the energy flowing between you.

♥ Don't change the subject or talk about things other than what is right in front of you. This time of stillness is a time to bask in the beauty of simply being together.

♥ Spend time connecting through your eyes.

Being Overwhelmed by Stories

Dear Darius,

It's the morning of my birthday. I roll over and try to get your limp hands to hold me. Your fingers have a meekness that I don't understand. I reach out to you with words, with hands, with lips and finally with tears. Nothing reaches you. I want to be celebrated. I thought today of all days that you'd come back. That life would flood back into your eyes and love back into your heart.

Six months with the shell of who you once were is just too much for me to bear today of all days. You pick up your phone and start texting. Still looking at your phone you tell me you want to break up. My tears turn to sobs.

"Are you fucking kidding me? It's my birthday!"

You look up from your phone for a moment, your eyes laced with numbness, and go back to texting.

"Why are you breaking up with me?"

My questions are only met with a statement.

"I need you to give me a ride so I can get off this island."

We've been together two years, and the morning of my birthday I'm cut loose without explanation. I am left with a tornado of questions and emotions all spinning together making me dizzy.

Through a kaleidoscope of tears, I drive you into town so you can catch a ferry back to our home in Seattle. Your silence slices through me. Your abruptness of ending cuts into me.

You tell me you want me to move all my stuff out of our house, and I have two days to do it. And that you don't want to see me or talk to me anymore.

The end of us is so sudden and unexpected and cold, I have to constantly fight off stories. My mind wants to spin a web of ten thousand reasons why you shut me out. I am constantly grappling, "What did I do wrong?" and its sidekick, "Maybe he'll come back." And I am perpetually pummeled by the worst villain of all: "How could I have been with someone who treated me so badly?"

Our time together was so much about integrating the darkness. Now here I am left with nothing but stories that multiply until they become a sticky ball of shadows. The worst part is not being able to talk to you. Here I am writing you a letter you'll never get and calling on all my superpowers to ward off the stories I want to create of why you left.

Why?

Kamala

We can never truly know why others do what they do. All we can know is we never know. We can spend days, weeks or lifetimes trying to understand why someone else hurt us or how the next person is going to hurt us. We can try to protect ourselves from pain, but we can't. We are human. Pain happens. People will hurt us and we will hurt others. But the thing that causes the most pain is shutting ourselves off from love.

Love is something that can't be taken away. When someone leaves, it's incredibly painful that they are no longer here to love us. But no one has the power to take away our love. Even if they leave, we still have the power to love them. It is the stories we create that make us feel separate from love. When we interrupt the stories before they take over our minds, we give ourselves a real chance at love - love that can't be broken no matter what others are doing.

At any moment, feel free to interrupt yourself. Just because you have a story, thought, or feeling doesn't mean you have to see it through to the brutal end. When you think or feel something about yourself or your partner that doesn't feel absolutely amazing, then you don't have to finish it. Our minds are constantly moving us away from love. As we interrupt our stories, and check out what is happening in the moment, we train our minds to choose loving thoughts instead.

Roadmap to Intimacy—Interrupting Consuming Thoughts

1. Journal about or share with a partner something that has been consuming your thoughts or a problem you keep thinking about. Give yourself ten full minutes to get it all out.

2. Put on some music and let yourself fill your space with sound and movement. Do a dance of how this problem moves through your body.

3. For the next twenty-four hours, notice whenever that repetitive thought comes up. Catch yourself in the act of thinking about it. Whenever it comes up adjust your body to a new position. If you're walking shake yourself out or if you're driving lean back more.

   The key is not to get frustrated with your thoughts, but to notice they are there. Simply adjust your body to release the experience and to think something different. Even if the thought comes back a minute from now, for this moment choose something else.

4. If you have trouble catching yourself creating stories, set a timer to go off every ten minutes and notice what your thoughts are doing.

Wanting to Have It All Figured Out

Dear Darius,

I've moved into a community house with four fierce-hearted men, and a year and a half long devotion to an immersion into Tantra. I am living with my mentor and we all dive into a sort of forced closeness that brings up everything that is still standing in between us and love.

So often I've wished I could talk with you about what happened between us, and why, after two years, you shut me out. The strength and love of community has helped me to navigate my murky waters within. Each man in the house seems to bring a wild and much needed gift that I can't help but be transformed by.

The bonds I am growing with the women from the larger community are helping me to need women in ways I never have. The woman I feel closest with is Tonya. When I look into her, it's like staring into a deep, multi-dimensional mirror. I see the most brilliant and powerful parts of myself. With a glance, we speak in a language that words could never reach. I feel more closeness and trust to her than I've had with any other woman.

You've reached out to me because, of course, you want

something. The Tantra immersion is happening in the community house where I'm living, and you want in. I want love to be bigger than my pain. You and I meet, and it's magical. Your heart is beaming at full strength, and I feel swept away in the potency of your love. I feel like I can tap into the bigger love and let you in.

The next day, in the tantric classroom, ten men and ten women get naked together. I look at you from across the circle, delighted by my ability to be such an evolved being that I can sit here with you after everything we've been through. Your heart is so open and beautiful in this circle of our community.

The next time we're alone together, it's a different story. You're as cold and distant as the day you left. I don't understand your incongruence. You have a pattern of being profoundly open and loving, but when you get what you want, you shut off like a vacuum seal on a submarine. I wish you were consistently kind, even after you get what you want,

You must be like a spider. I feel like I get caught up in your web, and as soon as you suck all you can, you move on to the next prey. After experiencing your coldness, being in the Tantric classroom with you is a constant struggle to regulate my own nervous system. In a particularly sensual exercise, I see you latch onto Tonya. I turn my back to try and block out what I'm seeing, but I can feel her getting spun up in your web from across the room. I want to scream at you, "Leave her alone! Anyone but her!"

I try to breathe. I try to calm myself down. But I'm shoved over the edge. Panic floods through every cell like a red alert. I want, more than anything, to run as far and fast away from this place as I can. I can't do this. I can't see you latching on to my friends. I can't witness you draining the life out of anyone else.

Now every time I see you, it's followed by a panic attack that no amount of forgiveness or logic can soothe. Tonya reassures me that she's not interested in you, but as time tells that's not the case. You've already latched on to her, and finally, with a shaky voice, she confesses that she's moving forward with you.

I don't feel strong enough to be near her. You're a spider, and everything you touch is laced with a sticky invisible thread, and now that thread is spun around her so tightly, I feel I can't access her. It hurts, but I have to let her go as a friend right now.

The moment I realize that you're most likely an undiagnosed narcissist, I feel like I can forgive myself. It's a tricky disease that some of the most skilled therapists have trouble detecting. I forgive myself for getting caught in your web. I forgive Tonya for falling for the same trap. And I forgive you for doing your best with the thickness of a mental disorder coating your world.

Forgiveness is not enough to make me want to toss my arms around you and Tonya. I don't have the answer to what is.

Everything that's happened doesn't exactly inspire friendship, but you and Tonya are both woven into my world. I want to be such a master at intimacy, that I feel nothing but love. That's not where I'm at though. The only thing I know how to do is be gentle with where I am right now, and be open to change.

Right now the most loving thing I can do is walk away,

Kamala

Loving people can stir up the deepest pain. The more we can be kind and gentle with ourselves, the more we give ourselves a real chance at love. Life and love is messy, and we can't shield ourselves from being hurt. What we can do is make a fierce commitment to be here for ourselves no matter what. When we can show ourselves the tenderness and love that we want others to show us, then the pains which others can stir in us become increasingly less.

In order to treat ourselves with the sweetness that we need, we have to be able to be okay with where we are right now. We might not have all the answers, we might not be as evolved as we want to be, we might feel more hatred than we want to. But whereever we are right now is perfect. When we allow ourselves to be how we are right now, without struggling to change, we go easier on ourselves. We stop abandoning ourselves for not being the way we want to be. When we're not abandoning ourselves, then other people leaving us won't be seen as abandonment. When we stop hurting ourselves with self-attack, than we won't need to get so defensive when other people attack us.

Life, love, and healing is not about being better or getting over our issues and blowing through our pain, it's about being willing to accept all of it and allow the gates of who we truly are to open slowly and gently. If we are just trying to be perfect, we lose what is real. We risk hurting ourselves when we ignore where we are, and try to leap ahead to where we want to be. We risk pushing ourselves over the edge of what we can handle. When we're trying to be something different than what we are right now, then we don't actually give ourselves room to step forward. If we lose our tight grip on who we want to be, we can step into something far more spectacular and real—who we are becoming right now.

Trying to be who we want to be causes a disconnect from who we are in this moment. When we create a gap between where we are and where we want to be, we lose what the moment is offering us. We often think we need to be better or do better or achieve something and then we'll be an idealistic version of ourselves. The only way to close the gap between where we are and where we want to be is by fully accepting where we are right now. It is the space between who we are and who we want to be where we can grow into what we are becoming.

Roadmap to Intimacy—Embracing Imperfection

1. Make a list of all the things you find most disgusting, unappealing, ugly, and unlovable about who you are.

2. Go through the list one item at a time. With each ugly trait fill in the blank of this sentence:

   I am _____ (an ugly trait)

   So what?

   What's important right now is...

3. Remember to keep breathing and being aware of your body as you go through the list.

Summary & Quotes to Share

Intimacy calls us to embrace all the things about ourselves that we believe to be unlovable. If we can slow down, and create space for every aspect of ourselves, we can experience deeper levels of passion.

Inviting all of Yourself Forward
- ❖ Tending to our own pains, imperfections, and inadequacies allows us to unlock our original essence.
- ❖ Adding gratitude to our interactions amplifies connection, love, and unity.

The Shadow - Can I Love This Too?
- ❖ If we really want intimacy, the shadow needs to be brought into the light.
- ❖ We need to be willing to look at, show, and learn to love all the parts of ourselves we've kept hidden.
- ❖ When we withhold the shadows about ourselves, we create tension and a sense of separation.
- ❖ When we are willing to show the ugly stuff and express what is going on inside, people trust us more.

Making Space For All of You
- ❖ Creating intimacy with another requires us to open to ourselves and invites us to be wildly honest.

❧ We must be willing to show who we are moment by moment, however crazy or unlovable we believe ourselves it to be.

Delighting in Love Again

❧ When we are saturated in the thickness of a heavy situation, it's time to take a pause.

❧ When we don't make up our minds about "the way things are", and meet the world with curiosity in every moment, we get to meet each moment with fresh eyes.

❧ When we stay curious, our partners will have the opportunity to continually surprise us.

Self-Judgment

❧ The more we stop trying to hide the parts of ourselves that we don't like, the more free we feel.

❧ Self-judgment is a slippery snake that can subtly worm its way through, eating away at your relationships.

❧ When you're loving yourself, you'll feel confident, and confidence is the sexiest of all character traits.

Igniting Passion

❧ To experience profound levels of pleasure and presence with another, we must slow down, breathe, and give our bodies a chance to feel all the subtle and sensuous sensations it's capable of.

❧ When we let our breath softly flow to every cell, it can create an organic and deeply intimate experience with ourselves.

Being Overwhelmed by Stories

❧ When we interrupt the stories before they take over our minds, we give ourselves a real chance at love - love that can't be broken no matter what others are doing.

❧ As we interrupt our stories, and check out what is happening in the moment, we train our minds to choose loving thoughts.

Wanting to Have It All Figured Out

❧ When we can show ourselves the tenderness and love that we want others to show us, then the pains which others can stir in us become increasingly less.

❧ Healing is not about being better or getting over our issues; it's about being willing to accept all of it and allow the gates of who we are to open slowly and gently.

❧ The only way to close the gap between where we are and where we want to be is by fully accepting where we are right now.

❧ Trying to be who we want to be causes a disconnect from who we are in this moment.

✉ Share on Facebook and Tweet @KamalaChambers

SEVEN

ADAM

Deeply Connecting to Yourself and Your Partner

We met in Guatemala. I went there on a whim, and it seemed the whole purpose of flying to Guatemala was to meet Adam. He had practically been in my backyard all along, living just a three and a half hour drive and a boarder crossing away, but we had to make the six thousand mile journey to find each other.

In the magical days we spent falling in love in Guatemala, it was as though the bliss between Adam and I took all the pieces of my broken heart and glued them back together with love. We parted without knowing if we'd ever see each other again. But our connection between us was too strong to ignore. Once we were both back home, we continued to see each other.

Adam and I were different kinds of creatures, I was immersed in a community and mentorship doing Tantra work. Adam was an uncomplicated Canadian, who liked playing baseball and drinking beer. Yet somehow, Adam had a way of embracing all of who I was. He showed me how to love myself more fully.

Adam and I traveled and went on adventures together and delighted in the joys of being amazingly good to each other. Adam didn't want to move to the United States. I didn't want to move to Canada. We wouldn't have fit into each other's worlds. So we made a plan to move to an entirely new country and create a life that both Adam and I could fit into. Through our journey together, I found lasting love. What I discovered with Adam was an unending partnership and love affair that can never be broken.

Through the lessons and roadmaps in this chapter, I encourage you to dive deep within the well of yourself to find the connection and lasting love you so deeply deserve.

Others Help Us to Love Ourselves

Dear Adam,

I haven't seen my buddy Noah in months, but he calls me up and says, "Let's take a trip somewhere." I don't know why I choose the destination I do, but a week later we fly to Mexico, and a week after, we're in Guatemala. Maybe we flew all this way just so you and I could meet.

The first time I see you, I know I want you. I'm sitting on Noah's lap scoping out the crowded hostel. He asks if there is anyone I'm into here. I point to you.

That guy!

The love between you and I is insistent and grows with an effortless ease, as though we are simply reading the pages of a romance novel. We meet on Flores, an island in the middle of a lake, deep in the mysteries of Guatemala. We head into the night, walking in the moonlight over Flores' cobbled streets. I lay your towel down on the wet uneven boards of a dock. We lay there on that crooked surface, under that moon, next to that lake, holding each other. In the distance sounds of cats fighting, dogs barking, roosters crowing, and howler monkeys howling fill the gaps of quiet. Our kisses begin slowly and move deeper into passion. Our bodies rocking on the shifting dock.

Overheated by passion, I break away from you and dip my toe in the lake. The water wraps around my foot like a warm mouth. I strip my clothes effortlessly and dive in. I watch you hesitate with your hands around the waistband of your boxers. You drop them and dive in to meet me. The water feels warm and thick like heated milk. We swim around one another. Our bodies brushing together. Our lips touching. I feel the strength of you. The hardness of you.

Part of me wants to stay here all night, watch the sun rise over the mountains while we teach one another about pleasure. Instead, we dress and walk back to my hostel.

I want you, and it isn't until we spend the entire next day on the bus together that I really feel the depth of you. Eight hours later, we arrive in Lanquin for four days that last an eternity. We make love without having sex. Our touch plays between soft, sensual and loving to rough and wrestling. Our eyes meet again and again in love. In those moments all resistances melt. I choose to love you all the way through. Each new glance, touch, and taste is laced with even more love than the last.

When we're not loving on each other in bed, we hurl ourselves into adventures. At the top of a waterfall we stop to take in the world. The rushing water. The green. The beauty. The stillness. As I am saturated by this moment, you're idle nearby as if standing guard. My eyes tear and I know I am right where I need to be. I know everything will be more than okay; that everything I've been through, all the heartache has led me right here and right here is perfect. Right here reminds me that it will all work out just fine. The knowing, carried in these waters, moves into my blood and I feel that knowing seep into my future and transform my past.

Whatever is to come, I will be able to handle it with more grace than before. Yes, I have had my heart broken, but I refuse to be broken by it. Here in this land of magic, with a new love shining on me, I choose to be undefended. I choose not to be careful with my heart and instead say, "I love you," and mean it. To reach out when I want to. To show weakness and allow myself to shed tears when I am overwhelmed with beauty. To laugh too wildly when I don't know what else to do. Part of me wants to keep you in Guatemala and never break the spell of such a great love.

When we return, the laughter doesn't stop until we are too cracked open by love and tears flow between us. We are amazed by the depth we feel toward one another and cradle each other in sweet bliss. We shower together and feel the heat of each other's bodies as we look over the dark jungle. The next day we both know it's our last, and most of the day is spent in bed. Crying on one another and laughing until I'm ejaculating more times than

I can count. I feel dizzy with pleasure.

Your hands are inside me massaging every point of pressure possible. I cum until the sheets are soaked through. I cum until the mattress is soggy. With each new orgasm a new space opens inside of me.

We go out to town to find dinner and as we walk the muddy road hand-in-hand elated and relaxed, suddenly an overwhelming feeling of nausea consumes me. Without warning, I nearly puke. I do not tell you this, but I feel that there is some evil within me trying to be released. I want to pray. I want to remove whatever entity has been locked inside of me. We continue to wander the streets, mostly empty with all the battered shops closed.

I am overwhelmed with nausea and fear I might faint. I don't know this culture or this country and being a woman I have so much more to lose then being robbed. I'm nervous for you. You hold me tight as we walk the streets. I hear most of the crime here happens because possessiveness of women. The only food we find is a small cart selling French fries and chicken in plastic sacks. We sit in a courtyard park. Mangy dogs sniff around us. Black plastic tarps cover the streets. It is so filthy and rural. Nearby there is romantic music in the air and it contrasts with the ugliness around us.

You look at me with all the love in the world and I begin to weep softly. How can I be so loved? All the pain, hardness and heartbreak I've been through has cracked me open and here you are filling in all those spaces in me with love. As you hold me, a tiny dog starts to eat your French fries and a small boy with a wild toothless grin appears from the night and tosses rocks at the sad puppy. It yelps and scurries away. This boy seems so pleased with himself. An act of kindness for us. A brutal act toward the dog.

You take my hand and we dance slightly to the music. The contrast of beauty and ugliness overwhelms me. I want nothing more than to dance with you, but the evil stirring inside me turns to fear when a few men enter the courtyard. I don't want trouble so I pull you back toward home. I nearly faint in the mud but you catch me and support my limp body.

Back in bed, I am delirious as you hold me. I'm on a rocking ship and can't seem to fend off sharks and jellyfish. I am babbling and shaking violently and confused. You let out a cougar growl and the visions of being attacked by the sharks and jellyfish start to part. The animals chasing me run from your growls. I drift off to your sporadic snarls keeping the hallucinations away.

I wake up screaming, "I have to get off this ship!" and start to vomit on the amrita soaked sheets crumpled on the floor beside me. You stroke my back and promise I'll be okay. I puke until there's nothing left inside me. I try to collect the massive vomit and cum soaked sheets but you stop me. You move into one of those critical moments when time stands still. I know you have a choice. You have both hands on the outside of the sheets. I wonder what you're going to choose. Stay on this ride with me or get off while it's gross. In both arms, you scoop up the weight of my sickness and carry it outside. I'm too weak to protest. In that moment I couldn't have loved you more.

You tend to me until I'm clean enough to sleep again. I try to apologize and you say, "I take the good with the bad."

Any doubts that were hidden within me that your love is real are washed out as you say, "There is still nowhere else that I'd rather be."

This kind of realness reveals a small box in my chest. Something that has been hidden from me until this moment of defenselessness. This tenderness. I see myself in all new ways. I am broken opened and healed.

The sickness is my final purge. You came into my life like a tidal wave of love and transformed me. Showed me all the goodness in myself. Taught me what it's like to be loved to the core. Reminded me of myself. Introduced me to me again. In our last hours together, I purge whatever sickness I had within me. Cleared it out to make room. Purged out the neediness and the hurt and the longing and made space again for all this love to continue to bloom within.

The next morning you have to catch your bus toward a flight out of here. However weak and sick I feel before you leave, you whisper in my ear, "I want to give you my entire body, mind, and heart. You already have my heart and most of my body." I convulsed slightly at the thought of this as your warm breath slips out of your mouth.

As you turn to walk out of our dorm room, I whisper, "I love you". My trembling voice muted by sickness. You don't turn back. You don't hear me, but I know you already know.

I fall into a deep feverish sleep,

Kamala

The quality of love you're drawing into your life directly reflects how well you love yourself. If we're not getting the quality and kind of love we want, then we can use this as a diagnostic for what kind of love we can give ourselves. If we are attracting people who aren't able to show us the kind of love we want, we can first identify what it is that we are wanting, and look for ways to give it to ourselves. The people we draw into our lives are brilliant mirrors for how deserving we feel to receive love.

This doesn't mean that we don't need anyone and we should be able to give all the love we ever need to ourselves. It's just an invitation to love ourselves better. We do need others. Others show us where we do not love ourselves, and teach us how to love ourselves better. We can know the ways we're not loving ourselves enough by what we feel is missing in our interactions with others. And we can learn how to love ourselves better by seeing how other people love us.

People may be able to love the things about ourselves that we see as unlovable. Others can remind us of how special we are. When we allow others to love us, they can show us more ways to love ourselves. As we open more to receive love from others, we can deepen our connections to ourselves.

When we expand into the sense of connection within, we can rest in center of who we are. If we don't start at our own center, there is no room for deeper bonding.

Our center means that we are not making the experience about the other person, our attraction to them, our desire, or even about our relationship to them. To access our center all we need is to open to love and feel ourselves. When we feel ourselves, we don't lean out of our center, desperate to receive love. We can simply relax into who we are and open the gates for others to come in and give love to us.

Roadmap to Intimacy—Adore Yourself

In your journal, write down all the ways you want to be loved on the left hand side of the page. On the right hand side of the page, write down one thing you can do to give that kind of love to yourself.

Example:

How I want to be loved:	What I can do to give myself that love:
I want to feel adored.	Cook myself a fancy dinner.
I want to feel heard.	Spend some time writing or audio journaling.
I want more pleasure.	Touch myself the way I want another to touch me.

Deeply Connect to Yourself and Your Partner

Dear Adam,

After Guatemala, we had no idea if we'd see each other again. After we realize we're just three and a half hours and a boarder crossing away, we can't resist. When you visit, I am surprised by your ability to step into some of the tantric work we're doing. You melt in for just a few days at a time with a grace I've never seen a "normal" person do. I say normal because the esoteric, personal growth, spiritual and new age has no frame of reference in your world. I can use words like chakras or kundalini or Tantra and you really have no idea what I'm talking about. Yet, you don't need the teachings and the language behind it all. You just seem to get it. You say, "Yes," to experiences with the curiosity of a child.

I feel you inside me constantly. It helps with the distance since we only get to see each other every few weeks. The deeper I go on my tantric path, the more I long to share this work with a partner. We're not partners and I know that. I'm your girlfriend. You're more like a container for my growth as opposed to someone who rises up to meet me and calls me into more powerful versions of myself. I love the gentleness of us and the ease of us. And, sure, shit comes up, but we're able to ride it out until we're giving each other high-fives at how we made it through the hard shit.

We go on seemingly endless adventures together. With you I find the calm from the storm of my home life. At home, there is no real place to hide. There is a fury of emotion, and every time I creep out of my room, I seem to be met with a mirror to look deeper into myself. With you, and our adventures, I find a sacred pause from the seemingly impossible growth of living and working with a community of people committed to burning all the way through love.

I move closer into you. I see our ability to move through the shit with grace as a sign that we can really make anything work together. The ease of us treats the symptom of my life overwhelmed. I feel like it would be easy to build a life together, but I fear a white picket life with you.

You are my calm in the storm,

Kamala

Being in love and having someone to be close with can be the most amazing feeling. Touch and sex can calm and relax the whole body. Physical closeness can be a great way to feel better. When life is out of balance, we seek ways to regain balance. We can use the bliss of being close with another as a way to feel balanced. And that's awesome.

We can lean into another person to help when we are overwhelmed. If we lean too far, it can put pressure on the other person. And if the other person pulls away, we can lose our balance. Going to others to help relieve our own pressure can be a great way to treat the symptom of stress. Using others to treat our symptoms is not too different than using pharmaceuticals to treat symptoms of disease. Some pharmaceuticals may relieve symptoms, but often don't treat the underlying issue. They're not designed to cure.

Leaning in is not a bad thing. We need people. We need love. And seeing ourselves lean can be an opportunity to see ways we can better love ourselves.

In situations where we are leaning into someone too much, ask:

What is it that I really need right now?
What is it that I am really wanting?
How can I decrease my own stress?

When you are leaning in or leaning away from someone too much, you're going to lose your center. If you are doing martial arts, your stance is one of the most important areas of focus. Your feet should be planted so no one will be able to knock you down. You stay rooted in yourself and people won't be able to pull you off your own center. Bend your knees and sink into your center of gravity so the other person can't toss you around.

When we physically adjust our bodies, we can emotionally and mentally adjust. The more solid we are in our stance, the more we can simply reflect and redirect the energy that is coming through. We have full control of how we want to be affected by another person. All that is required is that we be even more present with ourselves. More grounded. More prepared. Even more ready for what people are tossing at us.

We think we're "safe" if we are leaning in and ready to fight. We think we're safe if we are checking out and leaning away. But really, the only time we are truly safe is if we are aware and centered in our own bodies, right here in the moment.

Roadmap to Intimacy—How to Find Your Center

1. Stand up and lean forward until you feel like you might fall. Notice how you're bracing your body. Notice what happens within you. What sensations are happening in you?

2. Now lean as far back as you possibly can without falling. Notice how your body tenses to keep you up right.

3. Now, stand centered. Bend your knees. Feel your feet firmly planted on the ground. What does that feel like? How can you play with helping your body to feel even more supported while standing there?

4. Breathe deeply. Let your breath move all the way down into your feet. Really pay attention to how this feeling of centeredness feels in your body. This is a feeling you can keep coming back to. You can call upon it at any moment. This is something you can do no matter what anyone else is doing.

Radical Self-Love

Dear Adam,

We go to the Cayman Islands together and spend two weeks on beaches. The moment I meet your mom, I love her. When we walk out of the airport, she tosses her arms around you with a squeal and a squeeze that lasts so long it almost makes me (master cuddler) uncomfortable. She squeezes you so tight, tears spill out of my eyes. And her love doesn't quit. She keeps generously giving. Her love is so powerful it breaks me down. It's not that she smothers or is meek with you. She is a powerful woman with a generosity that extends to anyone who needs it. She has a seemingly endless amount to give and the way she loves you so fully and completely, is the way that I want to love you. I can see how you don't fully open to her love. I can see the huge task of having to hold back my own love because it's too similar to your mom's love that you have spent your teenage and adult life trying to fend off.

Maybe a man just can't fully let in that kind of love from his mother. Seeing how she loves you both hurts me and sets me free. I know that I can never fully love you the way I want to because it's too close to her kind of love. For months, I will cry every time I think of the way she loves you. This is truly one of the most inspiring displays I've ever come across.

When it's time to leave, she stays with us at the tiny airport until we board the plane. I can't stop crying. I can hardly look at her because I don't know how to say goodbye.

As we get on the plane, the captain comes over the intercom and says, "Adam and Kamala, I promised your mom I'd get you home safely. If you look out the window, she'll be waving goodbye."

From my window seat, I look out to see her standing there, arms high in the air, waving back and forth in a slow rhythm. My tears become quiet sobs. My heart breaks open. I hate saying goodbye, but I take the gift of the depth and freedom of love with me.

I've never seen love like this,

Kamala

Intimacy fully pivots on self-love. Yes, I know you've heard you have to love yourself before you can truly love another. Yes, you need to give yourself love and it all sounds great in theory. But I'm not here just to talk about loving yourself. I'm here to talk about having a wild love affair with yourself. Where you love yourself so much that you give to yourself fully and completely. Where you rise up and make a choice to stand by yourself no matter what. If you are so fully and completely with yourself, then you never have to worry whether someone will withdraw their love, or whether you'll lose yourself to love.

Much of your ability to relax into bliss depends on how much you can accept yourself. When difficult feelings arise, invite yourself to stay with them, experience them, and move through them. True intimacy can bring up deep emotion. Allow yourself to express it and be witnessed by your partner.

Your heart does not belong to you. You are simply the gatekeeper. Your heart is one tiny essential sliver of the living heart of this universe. Your heart is the missing piece of the puzzle. As gatekeeper, it is up to you to protect your heart from robbers. To keep it unburied. To keep the pulse flowing to the collective heart. All that you need to be is the gatekeeper, tending to the treasure that is your heart.

Roadmap to Intimacy—Self-Love

Make a list of twenty-five things you can do that help you to feel loved and adored.

For example:
- → Take a hot bath
- → Take myself out dancing
- → Go for a walk in nature
- → Cook myself a fancy dinner

Keep the list on your bathroom mirror, in your wallet or purse, or someplace you'll see it often. Whenever you want to feel loved, refer to the list, and do something that will helped you feel the love you desire.

Keep Opening

Dear Adam,

We talk about seeing each other more. I tell you I want to marry you. I tell you I want to try this thing out. We make a plan to move to Australia together after my Tantra mentorship in Bali. We both know that there is no way we can fit into each other's worlds, so we talk about creating our own world together. I can feel you holding back, but I stay quiet and wait for you to come around. I know time is running out for us to buy our visas and make a decision together.

I've fallen in love with a man named Miguel who understands the path I'm on. I am clear that I want to be with you, and I feel so relaxed to finally be loved by this other man man who rises up to meet me and calls me forward in ways you never have. My love for Miguel makes me love you more. I stop feeling desperate to gain your love. I stop feeling desperate to share my Tantric path with you because I feel like I can have that with Miguel and still stay true to us. I tell you about him, and as suspected, you are incredibly supportive and happy for me. You're not threatened, nor should you be.

Loving Miguel gives me a newfound confidence to go

after what I am truly wanting. What I want with you is your commitment to us. I want to know that you're going to rise up and meet me, and we're going to create a life together. You're holding back. It is time to make a decision about us and about going to Australia together. I'm coming to see you, and I need your clarity.

I feel the power of love surging through my body on the entire drive to you. Miguel, you, my community, and your mom have all been waking up parts of me like dominos. A path of love is blazed through me until I am fully resting in the most profound sense of self-love that I have ever felt. I feel the awesomeness of my spirit, the beauty of my body, the power of my heart and I know that I can truly do anything I want with my life. I fall all the way into love with myself and I spend the four hours driving to you in complete ecstasy.

When I arrive, I'm still buzzing from the amazement of the trek. As soon as I look into you, though, I feel you withhold. And your tight-lipped kisses tell me everything. We climb into bed together and talk about the life we want to create.

I breathe and keep opening to you and know this is a critical conversation that could either bust us into deeper commitment or fully break us apart. We talk until we are both exhausted and fall into a deep sleep together. When we awaken, we are both calm and holding each other gently. You say you feel our love is like a tether and most of the time you have the freedom to go wherever you want, but every once in a while you feel the tether is just not long enough.

Your idea of fun is bars and baseball games. We are different kinds of creatures. I try to protest. I tell you that I see how I've been putting pressure on you and wanting you to be able to fulfill my need for a partner who could do this work with me. But now I see I can have that with others outside of us and loosen my grip on my need for our love to rise up and meet me.

But it's too late. I realized how I've wanted to cram all my needs into our weekends together. I am a passionate person and I want to fully express that passion with you, which is hard to fit into the box of just a few days together. You say you're clear it's over, and I know that since we just awakened from slumber that this is truly the most clear you can be.

I feel the immediate stab of rejection. I pull away and step out into the moss in the tiny dress I am wearing. It's raining and I'm barefoot. The ground springs up to meet my feet with a surprising cushion of warmth. I lay on the damp earth and look at the snowcapped mountain peering through the swiftly moving clouds. The raindrops on my face and bare legs burn my skin. They bite and sting me like my emotions. Each droplet forces me into my body with a razor blade of reality. It's really over. The stories flood in…I have given so much for love and it keeps chewing me up and spitting me out and refuses to give me relief. I am flooded with rejection. And then something rises up from deep within and wraps around me.

Kamala, I'm not going to hurt you.
I'm not going to leave you.
I've got you.
I hear it as clearly as if I'm speaking out loud to myself.

I feel myself here with me in a way I've never felt before. I know for a fact that this time I'm going to be okay—more than okay. I am here with me and I'm not going anywhere. Sometimes I may forget how deeply I love myself. Sometimes I may give too much to a relationship and forget how much I am here with me. With that will come self-loathing again. But I know without a shadow of a doubt that I will be here for me and that love is not going away.

I step into the warmth of your house. I breathe your smell in deeply, knowing it's going to be the last time I enter your door. You're still in bed. I wordlessly crawl to you. I can feel you study me tentatively—not knowing what is coming next.

"Thank you for Guatemala. Thank you for the Cayman Islands. Thank you for California," the gratitude spills out of me until our tears meld together.

"Thank you for your mom," this sends us both into sobs.

We do what we do so well, we arrive back at love. Our appreciation turns to wet salty kisses. I whisper to you, "Make love to me one last time." And you do. You peel me away and you enter me with a calm, quiet grace. The infinity of love that we made together rushes through our bodies. With each gentle thrust, I say goodbye a little more and say hello to myself. I allow our entire time together to flood through my entire being and I know that what we have can't be taken away.

I spend the night. At dawn you leave me in your bed. You cry and kiss me and tell me once again that I have been the best thing that has ever happened to you. I stay quiet and look into you, wordless and unblinking, with my big glossed over blueness. You walk out the door and I am left with just me, and a long contemplative drive home.

As I drive out of the deep and beautiful valley you live in, I feel lightness in my heart. The drive is as dramatic and illuminating as it's ever been. The long sweeping views of salty inlets and islands and thick green mountains bare the newness that only leaving something behind brings. The sporadic rains and sunbursts seem to perfectly match my moods.

I feel like I am free falling into the unknown. I have no idea what the future brings, but I am clear on a few things…I know I love myself more than I ever have before. I know I'm buying a one-way ticket to Asia. I know that I'm in love with another man. And I know that at the end of this drive, he'll be there.

On the narrow drastic drop off of the Sea to Sky Highway, I scale my eyes between the road and the views and know that everything is going to be all right. No matter what happens or who I end up with, I'm with me. I am committed to me. I'm filled up by the greatest partnership I've ever know...the one with myself.

Deeply in love,

Kamala

Even in the face of what seems like rejection, resentment, or attack, we have a choice to either keep opening or contracting. We can perpetually invite ourselves to open and move closer to ourselves. Other people "hurting you" is your invitation to move closer to yourself.

What does it feel like in your body when someone
  says something hurtful?
Is there a wave of pain, or a stabbing sensation, or
  even a numbness?

Whatever it is, your only job is to feel it and be with it. It doesn't need to be changed or different, it just needs your attention. We often don't want to feel these things because, let's face it, they hurt. If we spend our time running away from the pain, we can never fully be present with another or ourselves and never really experience true intimacy.

When you feel hurt by what someone says, I invite you to just feel what you are experiencing in your body. There is no need to create stories about why that pain is there or figure out why you are hurting. The only thing you have to do is be there with yourself and your own sensations.

You have the choice to keep opening. Don't try to force yourself to move out of the experience, but open to the experience you are having. You are free because you always have the choice of how deeply you want to keep opening. You are free because you can choose what you will feel and what you won't. The more you open yourself to experience, the freer you will be.

We all want to be fully received. I have learned through all my relationships, men have left because I wasn't fully receiving them. They left because I wasn't creating the space for them to step into. This is not a self-attack. There were some things I didn't want to open to. There were some things I wasn't willing to fully receive. Those relationships didn't stand a chance. Before getting into a relationship, it's good to know what you absolutely are not willing to open to and receive.

The more you relax and open to who you are, the more you reflect that out to the world. You will attract people who mirror that reflection. When you dissolve your stories about how others should be or how you need to be, trust becomes irrelevant. If you are really present with what people are bringing through and who they are moment by moment, you won't be disappointed about how they are are acting.

Adam didn't feel fully received. And although we love each other deeply, I just couldn't open fully to him. It's still something I hadn't opened in myself, and I may never get there, and that's okay. I'm not bad or wrong for not being able to fully open to something. I get to discern what I want to open to. And the more I open, the easier it is.

When we take the pressure off the world to act according to our belief systems, we relieve a ton of pressure and can actually show up for how people are moment by moment. Intimacy is about choosing to fully embrace in the moment.

When we have stories about how our man or woman needs to show up, we lose sight of who they are. We create separation. Instead of trying to manage other people to show up the way we want them to, we simply need to adjust ourselves to show up. Our ability to step into what we are wanting creates an invitation for others to meet us there.

Everything is in a state of resonance, so people will either step up to resonate with you or they'll shake loose. I know it's terrifying to risk losing people. If we fully step into who we are, we risk someone not being able to meet us there. To keep ourselves small in order to stay with someone is the biggest disservice we can do for that person. By keeping ourselves small, we invite them to keep playing small. If we rise up and fully step into what we are wanting within ourselves, the person we love is also invited to rise up. Love the person you're with enough to fully come into yourself. Romance and love affairs and even marriages come and go. The only relationship you are guaranteed to have for the rest of your life is the one with yourself. You might as well try to make it work.

The game many of us play is trying to get other people to see us as lovable, beautiful, vibrant, powerful...the list goes on. But when we fully engage with ourselves and fully step into who we are, we stop trying to get the other to see us as what we want to be. You can try to be seductive. You can try to show only your pretty parts, but people don't want to be seduced. People want to move all the way through you.

We all want to be fully met. We all want to fully open and be opened. When you have two people who aren't opening, you have a woman who is desperate for a man to open her and a man who is hungry to pound her into openness so she can fully receive him.

What is the alternative? Fully open yourself and you won't have to try to seduce people to come closer. Fully open yourself and you won't be desperate or starved to draw someone in who can open you or fully receive you. Open yourself and you will draw in people who are open, plugged in, and turned on by life. When you merge together, your openness will create even deeper openings.

After hearing my story of going from one man to the next, you might think, this book isn't about lasting intimacy. But it is. You can have lasting intimacy no matter who is in front of you. You can drop into an experience of unity and deep presence with yourself.

The amount of love and intimacy you can hold all depends on how present you can be. How much can you show up for yourself, your lover, a checkout clerk, and the tree you're passing? The more you can open to what is in front of you and inside of you, the richer the possibility of love. When someone "takes their love away," we hurt because we stop being present to what's there. We instead hold onto the memories and feelings.

When we go through a process of "losing" with presence to whatever pain or discomfort is showing up, our bodies, minds and hearts naturally fill with love. We are brought here to remember that we are all God experiencing itself. The only thing that is real in this world is the relationships we have because in those relationships we get to be God and see God and experience ourselves through the mirrors of others.

Something happens when the heart breaks open wide. The veil between total love and deep desperation breaks down. If we love deeply enough, we may find our hearts aching. In loving, we are also letting go. Only love this deep understands that you cannot hold onto it. The very act of clinging to love, defies it. There is only so long you can hold the sweet nectar of love in your mouth before you have to swallow it, and your pallet is only left with the memory of its flavors. Drink it in and let love become a part of you.

Summary & Quotes to Share

To connect deeply with others, we are required to radically love ourselves.

Others Help Us to Love Ourselves

- ❖ If we're not getting the quality and kind of love we want, then we can use this as a diagnostic for what kind of love we can give ourselves.

- ❖ Others show us where we do not love ourselves, and teach us how to love ourselves better.

- ❖ When we feel ourselves, we don't lean out of our center, desperate to receive love.

Deeply Connect to Yourself and Your Partner

- ❖ When we physically adjust our bodies, we can emotionally and mentally adjust.

- ❖ The only time we are truly safe is if we are aware and centered in our own bodies, right here in the moment.

Radical Self-Love

❖ If you are with yourself, then you never have to worry whether someone will withdraw their love, or whether you'll lose yourself to love.

❖ Much of your ability to relax into bliss depends on how much you can accept yourself.

Keep Opening

❖ Even in the face of what seems like rejection, resentment, or attack, we have a choice to open or contract.

❖ When we dissolve our stories about how others should be or how we need to be, trust becomes irrelevant.

❖ The only relationship you are guaranteed to have for the rest of your life is the one with yourself.

✉ Share on Facebook and Tweet @KamalaChambers

Acknowledgements

Creating this book has been a tremendous journey of self-exploration. I have utilized my own life experiences and combined them with a variety of teachings that come from many paths of study. This book includes teachings from the Institute for Integrative Nutrition, the Earth Walk Institute of Healing Arts, and mentors Dayna Lowe, Gayle Alizar, and David Cates.

As a teacher, I acknowledge that no teacher finds his or her way without the support of other teachers. One of those key teachers for me has been Master Tantra Teacher, David Cates. As a student of his work, he has helped me slow down, breath, feel, and find my way deeper into love. Thank you, David, for allowing me to share excerpts of your teachings in this book. For anyone seeking a deeper understanding of Tantra in its most simple and profound form, I highly recommend seizing the rare opportunity to work with David Cates.

I would like to thank my community as a whole for your support. The names are too many to mention here, but I am deeply grateful for you.

I am grateful for friends who have shared with me special lessons that are integrated into this book. Thank you Buster Jonas Rådvik for your knowledge on regulating the nervous system. Yuri for your profoundly disgusting methods that helped me to learn about dispelling shame. Zachary Fulton for your wildly shamanic openings that have helped me to delight in discovering newness in each moment.

Truly my greatest supporter through the process of writing this book was Luis Congdon. You supported me through the emotional turrets of reliving my past relationships. You helped me with editing, bringing me countless meals, loving me up, giving me pep-talks, encouraging me when I wanted to give up. You picked up the slack when the process consumed me. Your love and support is truly inspiring. A million times thank you.

Thank you Joshua Rosenthal with the Institute for Integrative Nutrition and Lindsey Smith with Promoting Natural Health. You have been key players in keeping me on track to see this book through all the way to publication.

Thank you immensely to Jim Carroll with J Shu Images for your incredible photography skills, laughter, wisdom, and shooting the images on the cover of this book. And for Amie Olson for your cover design skills.

Thank you to my publisher Promoting Natural Health. For anyone seeking support to be published, I highly recommend them.

I would also like to make a special acknowledgement to those people who have taken time to read chapters and discuss this book with me. Thank you Sue, Luis, Jenny, Alexandra, Sunday, Rebecca, Lindsey, Amy, Virginia,

Hafizullah, Raya, Rick, Kathy, Mark, Veenu, David, Gloria, Deborah, and Kristen…Thank you all for your generosity in reading the rawest forms of this work.

An acknowledgment page would not be complete if I did not include the key people in my life who made my existence possible—those people being my parents. Thank you Mom and Pop. Mom you have provided for me a great freedom to follow my own flow and you have always encouraged me to find my own path—even if it's not the accepted norm. Pop, although I'm not sure you'll feel comfortable reading this book, I want to acknowledge you none-the-less. Your love and acceptance helps me to know that anything is possible.

The names of people who made this book possible could truly fill all the pages here. I just want to give a special shout out to the following people: Joshua, Abram, Stephen, Chetana, Mary, Noah, Alex B., Evernus, Maclean, David C. Jerimy, Ebony, Janice, Jannae, Gretchen, Shawn, Douglas, David T., Ally, Sydney, Rachel, Adele, Ko-Shin.

I want to give a huge thank you to Rebecca Gould for making a special contribution towards the launch of this book.